Heart in the Night

Printed in the United States of America.

Cover design by Barbara K. Donithan

Published by Gama Books, Inc.
2011

www.gamabooks.com

This book is offered exclusively at
www.gamabooks.com

For my father...

my dearest friend who came to me in a dream
after his passing and handed me a typewriter,

and for Brian...

a music instructor in Texas who experienced great
loss and gave me a reason to write again when I
was in "the in-between."

Heart in the Night

From Death to Rebirth
Experiencing Great Loss During the
End Times

KAREN BISHOP

CONTENTS

"When all the broken-hearted people living in the
world agree,

there will be an answer, let it be."

— Paul McCartney

"These things I have spoken unto you, that in me
ye might have peace. In the world ye shall have
tribulation: but be of good cheer; I have overcome
the world."

— John 16:33

PROLOGUE

SHE THOUGHT IF SHE COULD JUST keep on driving, she could get away from it. The night before, in a fit of desperation and finality, she packed up her car with some basic needs, preparing for her grand escape. Some audio books, Paul Newman's dark chocolate peanut butter cups, zero calorie drinks in her favorite pear flavor, and as an afterthought, a new map of the US— in case she needed some indication of where she was. Her basic needs had become very simple.

As her car followed the blacktop mile after mile, spread out as far and wide as one could see, were vast green pastures interspersed with small lakes, and an occasional barn with an accompanying farmhouse. Trying to distract herself, she loaded cd after cd of an audio book into her stereo system in an attempt to keep her wandering mind anchored to something—

anything to take her somewhere else. The melodic voice of the narrator had begun to lull her into a state of calm, just about the time she reached the wide-open spaces of Oklahoma.

She had been driving since sunup in a near trance, and now that mid-day had arrived, her stomach reminded her that she was still alive and breathing. She needed fuel. Not wanting to eat, but yearning to fill up the empty space within her, she rolled down the windows of the car and breathed in deeply. The smell of green grass, damp from an early morning rain, and the faint lingering of honeysuckle brought a much needed comfort. With a sky so blue that it seemed to stretch to infinity, oh how she wished that all this alone could sustain her. She did not want to think about food.

Grrrrrrowl. Her stomach was talking again. It seemed to be asking for help, like a newborn unable to feed itself. Unable to ignore its demands, her stomach brought her back to the here and now—the small world of her car—her only world left now—the world of her immediate surroundings. "Well, Bernie," she said as she looked over her shoulder into the back of the car. "What do you think?" As was her normal way on long trips, she glanced into the back of her car, making sure that her small dog Bernie was comfortably settled in his crate. Her constant companion and closest friend, he was continually by her side. "Do you ever go anywhere without that dog, Laura?" her grandmother often chided her during their special time together. "You two are attached at the hip! It's a wonder he knows he is a dog at all!" Just two months earlier, her beloved grandmother and sweet soul mate, had passed away very suddenly in her sleep.

As Laura's gaze reached Bernie's usual spot in the back of the car, she was suddenly catapulted into her very new reality – a reality that had slowly and steadily arrived seemingly all on its own. Bernie had died a few days before…the last of her circle of loved ones to leave her. There was no crate, no familiar black and white face looking back at her, the same tussle of hair hanging over his right eye as his gaze so frequently met hers, tongue hanging out in a slow and easy pant, and no familiar smell of Bernie. She was now completely alone, bewildered, severed from the last of anything meaningful, and driving to who knew where in an attempt to free herself from heartbreak so deep, she wondered how she would ever survive.

. . .

1

THE METAPHYSICAL MUMBO JUMBO

THE EARTH HAS GONE MAD—where am I, anyway? How in the world did I get here?! Have I died and descended into hell and somehow never knew it? Why is this happening to me?! There is nothing to hold onto! Nothing makes any sense anymore! My spiritual beliefs have completely evaporated and left me stranded! I cannot connect to my higher power. No one sees me or acknowledges me—it is if I am invisible. Where did my job go? How can I ever earn a living again? The earth has become uninhabitable. Everything in my life has disappeared! I am completely powerless and lost, and no one cares! Who am I, anyway? I forgot who I used to be. I am not good at anything and have been reduced to nothing! I am treated as if I am insignificant when I used to be powerful and full of life! Everything has been taken from me! Nothing new is arriving and everything is going! The darkness seems to be taking the upper hand! Whose idea was this anyway?! Please take me back to the familiar—this feels horrible!!!

Have you ever felt like any of the above? Have you ever felt as if you were now somewhere strange and unfamiliar, with no remote sense of security or well-being? Have you ever wondered where anything or everything was going, as it seems so much is out of control, has lost its direction and most certainly its integrity?

Unless we have been held captive by a remote tribe in a third world country, or perhaps been chained to a chair watching *Gilligan's Island* re-runs with home food delivery, most of us undoubtedly sense that the planet earth is undergoing a massive change and restructuring. Something amazing, miraculous, and unstoppable is indeed occurring for us all. Age-old prophecies from the Bible, through the Mayan calendar, from Hopi tribes, to anything and everything relating to the cosmos and spiritual arenas have known this time was indeed a-comin'. Even if we are not an avid reader of any of these kinds of materials, and simply a resident on the planet earth, the times of change cannot go unnoticed.

Most prophesies and spiritual arenas seem to be conveying the same message — stating very simply that **the world is about to end.** Over. Caput. Dead. The world as we have known it for eons of time is about to exist no more. It is no wonder then, that so many are feeling insecure, frightened, lost, and confused. Who would not feel that way when all we have ever known is about to depart? But many of these ideologies also firmly express something more: **A new world is about to arrive.** It is not so much about the death of the old as it is about the arrival of the new. And this new world is intended to be much more spiritual and more highly evolved—with more love, caring, respect, and unity than we have ever known before. "The end" almost always precedes a leap in consciousness—a very new beginning into something much better than before.

Is anything and everything that is not spiritual or that does not come from love going to be punished and wiped off the face of the earth? Will there be judgment, wrath, and a separation of good and bad? Will there be pain, suffering, and massive loss? In the end, it is all a matter of personal interpretation and this is where the metaphysical aspect comes in.

When more light (or rather love, caring, respect, and unity— or more evolved energy) arrives, what is not like it departs, as light and dark cannot exist in the same space. This is a matter of simple physics and vibrational frequency. Higher and lower vibrational frequencies cannot share the same space, and light vibrates higher than darkness; they simply do not share the same food or source of life. Therefore, sharing the same space creates a massive mismatch and collision, and in the end, if light or a higher frequency predominates, darkness or a lower frequency, is forced to depart. The light then, pushes the dark to the surface for either a cleansing or a departure, which is essentially the same thing. So although it may appear that there is now more darkness than ever before, this is not what is actually occurring. What is visible now is simply what is left before a new world can arrive; and what is currently left at the time of this writing, is a very small thread indeed. This thread consists mostly of the old structures, ways of operation, and ultimately, what has been holding this planet together in the physical reality. It is no wonder then that many are feeling lost with nothing to hold onto, as it is simply reflective of what is left at the physical levels of reality.

"Uh, excuse me! It seems to me that the darkness, not the light, is what is pushing things out," you may be thinking. "I have been treated terribly and disrespected by those in charge of things. Not only that, but I have been shut down and unable to exist, as it seems the darkness has taken over the entire planet. I have absolutely nowhere to go and no way to earn a living, let alone live my life! I am virtually powerless, sitting here in a no space waiting for what, I do not know. I feel as if I have gone as far as I possibly could, and have now walked into a closet—and there are no side doors!"

Things are indeed in order, even if it does not feel like it at times. The old structures or old ways of operation will continue to be in place until there is something to replace them. If everything crashed at once, there would be chaos, fear, madness, and attempts made by something or anything to take over and fill that now empty space. As you will come to find out further along in this book, this has indeed occurred to a certain degree during some of the final phases (as we seesaw our way into the new), but as we move ever forward, this phenomenon eventually ceases to exist. And we can know as well, that the process is unfolding in a perfect and divine way— all the while being monitored and watched over by our heavenly protectors and caretakers from above.

A Long Story Short...Metaphysically Speaking

(If you are not a metaphysical person, you may want to skip these next few paragraphs. They may sound like some wild story from a strange book or at best written by a woman who has lost her marbles. But if you are metaphysically inclined, you will most likely relate to most of it, as it will feel like coming home with a strong connection to your soul. So hold your breath, or open your heart if you chose to read on.)

When this process of the end of the world began in earnest, around the year 2000, the earth was flooded with light in incremental waves that were spaced apart with perfect timing. This was so that each and every soul on the earth would have an opportunity to adjust to living with more light. Adjusting to more light was a brutal process, stretching many souls beyond what he or she believed they could endure, and taxing these individuals to their personal limits. With each wave of light came a massive purging and releasing of darker energy within each soul. Experiencing extreme fatigue, a loss of identity, numerous physical and emotional symptoms too strange to possibly understand, along with losses of jobs, physical residences, and loved ones, were common occurrences during these years (and *now*, these experiences are occurring for most everyone, as so much progress has been made—resulting in the arrival of the End Times). As these forerunner souls adjusted and aligned, there would then be a break in the process to allow for rest, or rebooting, as I often called it. During the rebooting process, lethargy, apathy, and listlessness would be present for a while, but the process would always continue on, as yet another wave of light would arrive and the purging and internal releasing would begin all over again.

In the beginning of this process, some souls were greatly affected by these waves of light, while others seemingly remained untouched. The souls who were affected first, came to the earth at this time specifically to assist in the transition of the old world to the new world. As these forerunner souls progressed in their ability to release more darkness within themselves, they were then able to embody more light, as there was now more "room" within them to house this new and higher vibration. This greatly assisted in bringing up the vibration of the planet. This process of pushing out the old to allow for the new is a predominant theme in regard to the creation of a new world and new reality. It applies to individuals, systems, societies, structures, and every existing thing on the planet.

For several years after the onset of waves of light arriving from "the outside," the spiritual evolutionary process of the planet (or grand plan) was adjusted according to how the light was being received. The intent and plan from the divine energies in charge of this process (or end of the old world so that a new world could arrive), was always to lovingly allow for as many souls as possible to have the opportunity to change, grow, expand, and otherwise embody more light within. As many souls as possible were wanted in this new and very different world that would soon unfold. In this way, more time was allotted than anticipated for this divine plan to unfold, as it was taking much longer for many souls to be willing to let go of old patterns and ego energy, and receive more light.

When the souls on the planet who *had* evolved—and/or who had chosen to undergo this massive and unusual process—had waited long enough (and a pivotal point was thought to have been reached)—the light arriving from "the outside" then ceased. It ceased because it was now time for the light to emit from each and every individual, or rather to come from "within" instead of from "without." At this time, is was intended that many souls come together, leaving egos at the door, in order to form a very new grid or rather the new foundation for a very new world. In this way, others arriving at a later time, would then have somewhere to go. But this did not occur. Attempts were made at connecting, but egos, arrogance, and fear were not left at the door. And because of this, there was nowhere left to go as the old world continued its collapse. This was a challenging time for many, as those who had dedicated themselves to this process were left hanging in mid-air—in a suspended animation—stuck in a birth canal—and with nothing to connect to and no foundation in place that would allow for creation. And for many old souls, creativity and a strong connection to the light are mandatory elements of life. These souls had indeed evolved beyond their current surroundings, creating a very challenging experience.

A predominance of light was always the intention, as in this atmosphere, the minority would always very naturally rise up in vibration and conform to the predominant energy of the light. This was the original divine plan, as it would offer much more ease, comfort, love, and gentleness than massive destruction, pain, and suffering. But as mentioned prior—the unforeseen and greatly unexpected occurred— and continued through many stages of the evolutionary process. The majority of souls residing on the planet chose to hold on fiercely to their old selves and lower vibrating energies, as their ego aspects were not willing to give up and depart. Fear took over, forcing the divine plan to be adjusted frequently so that those who had progressed could at least move forward into an arena that suited who and what they had now evolved into—as well as allowing other souls the opportunity to once again let go of the old. In this way, many distinct separations occurred so that the light would become the predominant energy within these separations, creating the air that it breathed.

Many other attempts and interventions were made by the divine as well, all too numerous, bizarre, and varied to list here. But with so much fear, corruption, and contamination affecting the intent of these interventions (all designed so that individuals would embody more light within), most all of these interventions and attempts resulted in failure. They sputtered, coughed and choked, and did not stick nor take hold as was hoped.

The intent then, for the years 2008, 2009, and especially 2010 was very focused on allowing all souls on the planet to embody light *within themselves*. This intent became much more aggressive in 2010, as it had not been producing the needed results in years prior. In this way, the loving souls who had evolved the most, would need to remove themselves, or at least stay back so that the remaining souls would not be tempted to take light from them, instead of propagating it within themselves. These more evolved souls remained sequestered, and were asked either consciously or at their subconscious soul levels, to cease giving love at this time. And what a challenge this was, as being loving and caring souls is what these souls were all about! During this time of removal, these loving and caring souls would be taken care of, having all needs strangely met, even though they had been prohibited from sharing their energy with others or becoming actively involved in the outside world.

When most of the light had removed itself, the very last tendrils of darkness comprised what was left. This darkness was left alone—so that it would eventually implode or destroy itself—or at least take notice. Imploding would greatly help the planet prepare for its next stage—which was all about turning itself inside out. In this way, the remaining darkness was allowed to go as far as it chose to go. At the same time, a wake-up call would hopefully sound for many remaining souls. It was hoped that they might recover themselves and realize that the planet was in grave danger, and cease to participate in its many lower vibrating ways—or at least actually notice that perhaps the world had seemingly gone mad. The empty spaces that were once filled by a light now departed, were now filled by a strange and confused darkness and seeming madness. In this way, "allowing" by the light was paramount here, as these remaining tendrils of darkness needed to find their own way. They had grossly disrespected and not "seen" those holding more light in times past—now they had to do it on their own. Would they find their way, or would they destroy themselves and implode? Either way would support the next phase of the process.

After much craziness, chaos, and numerous attempts and interventions from the light finally ceased, and the dust settled in the remaining months of 2010, each and every soul was then positioned in a space that now suited who and what they had finally evolved into. Because the spiritual evolutionary process had become corrupted at best, these souls found themselves scattered all over the planet, and with varying differences in their new purpose on Earth during this time. Many of the forerunner souls had recently and vehemently declared that they had had enough. They were indeed done. These souls were now poised to watch from the sidelines, as they had done all that was possible and could do no more. They were now placed in quiet and protective spaces, removed from the final days of the old world, and sequestered in pockets of their own desires until it was time to re-emerge once again—if they chose to re-emerge at all.

If this was not all far too exhausting and never-ending, a wonderful thing suddenly and finally happened. After the massive declaration of "enough!" from many of the forerunners, the light began to arrive from the "outside" once again. Earth changes and massive cleansings, loss of life, and new internal feelings of great love were now ever-present as the light began its new arrival. (How can loss of life and earth changes come from the light? You will indeed find out, further along in this book.) After several years of suspended animation, separations, "waiting," and numerous attempts at "nudging" the souls who were lagging behind, things finally began to move forward. The divine plan was indeed going ahead, no matter what the current state of the planet. For those who had emptied out the most, the newly arriving light, very gentle and very feminine, began to fill them up. A divine intervention and nudge from the "outside" was now in our midst. The light was finally here once again, if even from above. And all the hearts that had broken open from the pain and suffering of darkness, were now poised to be filled with a very new level of love.

13

So how then, does experiencing massive loss come into play with this big and newly formulated plan? And why is it even necessary at all? If you are still awake and your eyes have not glazed over, kindly read on, as it is all about the heart energy.

2

GOING, GOING... GONE

"WE NEED MORE PASTA!" shouted Raymond, Laura's lead cook. Today was busier than normal. At least 15 homeless people were lined up at the serving counter, irritably waiting for something to eat. "Laura, I thought you stocked up on everything yesterday?" an exasperated Raymond called over his shoulder as he rushed by. Laura wiped her brow, now heavy with perspiration from the hot kitchen. Donations for her non-profit homeless shelter and soup kitchen, The Helping Hand, *had been steadily dropping for the past six months. More than naught, each donation would arrive with a simple note: 'Wish it could be more, but things are tight right now.' And the contribution jar was no better.*

Ten years ago, she had fulfilled her life-long dream of starting a homeless shelter and soup kitchen. Beginning with a small kitchen and dining room, she had created her dream in her usual way by making it unique—very unlike any other organization out there. Several afternoons a week, local chefs would volunteer in the kitchen, creating unique and sumptuous meals for anyone who chose to enter the front door. All were welcome— local business people, town residents, and of course, the honored guests she created it all for in the first place—those who were unable to feed themselves. A contribution jar stood simply as the first stop along the serving counter so that anyone who could would have an opportunity to contribute to "the cause." Most working folks on their lunch breaks happily paid for their meals this way, as the excellent cuisine was known far and wide making The Helping Hand *a favorite spot to eat. Beginning with carefully planned fundraisers and additional funding from sporadic grants, these financial supports eventually became unnecessary, as* The Helping Hand *seemed to magically sustain itself as time went on. It wasn't long before Laura began turning away big name organizations offering support, as the community quickly and easily embraced her organization, swallowing it up as its own. To many a local resident, it had become the heart of the town.*

Slowly and steadily, Laura's non-profit grew and blossomed. As was her policy, those who received free meals almost daily, and were greatly in need of them, worked their way up the ladder of the organization. Sam, a man Laura had found sleeping outside the front door late one night, began working for his meals by sweeping the front walk, and was soon very proud to be cooking alongside some of the community's best and most talented chefs. As his self-esteem grew and he found new purpose, Sam eventually became her lead cook and was able to utilize his gifts of management along with a long dormant love for food. As more and more homeless and hungry people found their way to her door, she evolved and expanded, utilizing the building next door as a homeless shelter. Soon her organization could house and feed many in need, and could even provide necessary clothing for those with prospective job interviews. Just last year a reporter had visited The Helping Hand, *gathering information for a human-interest story. With a bright smile on his face, he left commenting, "The love, gratitude, and caring in this place is all-consuming. If this is what religion is like, I'm going to church!"*

Oh, how she longed for those days again—when so much of everything was different—when people were different, when the economy was different, when there were standards, and there was structure—not to mention morals and decency!

As Raymond rushed by, overloaded doing the job of three people now, Laura was again reminded of her lead cook Sam. She would often hear his familiar voice weaving in and out of garlic smells, the clanging of pots, and the sizzling of his specialty steak on the grill. He had been gone for several months now, and she dearly missed him. He had been returning home from a car show with his cousin when a storm hit. Trying to avoid a cyclist who was riding to shelter, their truck swerved out of control and hit a tree. Sam had broken his leg and sustained a head injury, leaving him with permanent memory loss, and a new and unfamiliar angry and hostile disposition. He became unable to provide his services to The Helping Hand. His steady, familiar, and comforting presence, with a joy and pleasure at being in the kitchen every afternoon, had abruptly ended.

And then as suddenly, the local businesses seemed to change their attitude toward The Helping Hand. "We just aren't comfortable having those vagrants so close to our places of business," Joe Hendle, the chamber president had said when he called one day. "Our business owners are afraid for their safety. And most of them now feel that those bottom-of-the-barrel people will drive away their customers. A few of our members even want to shut you down. We just cannot support you any longer. I'm sorry Laura, but times are different now, and we need all the business we can get."

Teri Jackson, the owner of the local hair salon, rarely missed her normal Wednesday lunch, and frequently brought along a friend or client. They loved the unusual cuisine, and their regular donations to the contribution jar had become a mainstay of support. Last week as Teri was *making a quick exit towards the front door after her lunch, she bumped into Laura outside the restroom door. "Oh, Laura," she mumbled under her breath. "I'm so sorry I can no longer donate every Wednesday. But, uh, knowing you, I know you will understand! Thanks for the great lunch! I am so grateful! See you next Wednesday!"*

Then there was Gary. Gary… the sensitive, caring, and sweet man who continually brought a humble and loving presence to her space. Gary had been a regular at The Helping Hand *for several years. Laura fondly remembered the day they first met. She had been setting up the lunch tables when she heard a light, barely audible tapping on the front window that overlooked the sidewalk along Hoover Street, the main drag in town. As her eyes looked up, standing on the sidewalk were two men distinctly different from one another. Bart, a familiar but sporadic visitor to* The Helping Hand, *loomed tall with a half grown face of whiskers, mussed head of black hair, and oil stained jeans that looked like they had become an appendage of his lean, long legs. Another man was standing next to him, small in stature, wearing a baseball cap with golden curls sprouting from beneath it, a t-shirt with a vibrant eagle image spreading across his chest as if to say, "I'm bigger and more powerful than you think!", and wearing an old pair of tennis shoes that seemed twice his size.*

Bart had continued to come and go, but Gary immediately settled in and took over the daily task of setting up the tables. A gentle and caring man, Laura had immediately taken to him. His gratitude for finding a safe and loving haven was always noticeable. But lately he seemed different. More interested in his own meal than taking his usual care with the table set ups, he began complaining to Laura. "Can you make me some tomato soup with a side salad?" he had requested the other day. And, "I've noticed you haven't been keeping up with new cot blankets. I need a new one. The one I have been using is too thin and I have been getting cold." Expecting her ever-loving and kind response, he had begun to take her for granted.

The clientele at The Helping Hand *had been changing too. There were more of them than ever before and most of the faces were new and unfamiliar. And along with these new faces came a new disrespect, arrogance, and demanding demeanor. One afternoon Laura heard a yelp from the yard backing up to the kitchen, and found her dog Bernie cowering under the stairs. Three young men who had just finished eating were throwing rotten oranges at Bernie, and laughing as they made their way home.*

Something had changed…and Laura felt as far away from her loving and familiar space as never before.

· · ·

When we finally get to a very new space after our journey of endings and massive loss, we can only blink our eyes in awe, look around in disbelief, and finally begin to understand why we had to go through all the pain and suffering of the past. And when we get to this space as well, the past suddenly seems very far away, as if it belonged to someone other than ourselves— as if it now belongs in another world entirely—a world that does not remotely resemble where we are now. Experiencing massive loss is a pivotal and substantial part of our spiritual evolutionary journey. And this aspect of the plan can be grueling, acutely challenging, devastatingly frightening, make us feel we are going mad, and create an emptiness and disconnect that we may never have experienced before.

The more we evolve, the more we lose what no longer fits us, so in a strange way, we could choose to look at this part of the process as a divine and strange compliment. Following the metaphysical concepts described in *Chapter 1*, we know that higher and lower vibrating frequencies cannot share the same space—hence, all the losses. But the more we lose and the more we choose to let go of, the more we will find ourselves in new and wonderful spaces that perfectly fit who, where, and what we have now evolved into. So although Laura experiences massive loss with immeasurable pain and suffering, after leaving everything behind, she eventually ends up in her heaven—experiencing a life and world that she could never have dreamed about in her wildest fantasies.

There is a very definitive reason that we have to let go of so much. We may let go of one thing here, and one thing there, but the process will continue on, and seemingly go on forever, until it is indeed quite done. *Everything* that no longer fits our new and divine selves must depart. This is especially true if we have agreed at our soul levels to be a part of this evolutionary process, and to experience it wholeheartedly. So in this way, *if we do not let go of everything we must let go of, we will only re-create more of the same when we begin anew.* It is vitally important then, that we start all over from scratch with a very new and alive rebirth in a very new and alive space, if we wish to reach a new and different reality altogether.

How do we know what to let go of, and how do we arrive in the space of no space where we have nothing left, before we can experience a dream life that now fits who we really and truly are? And how do we even know what our dream life is, anyway?

The Many Ways of Departure

We can leave the old world and our old lives behind in basically two ways: 1) We can consciously choose to walk away from jobs, people, residences, responsibilities, and the like, 2) or we can be removed through seemingly no fault or decision of our own. The former stems from our divine selves and the latter from a divine source outside of ourselves, which continues to watch over and protect us at all times. The more we have evolved, the more that these decisions will come from within, as we are slowly and surely *becoming* the divine source from above. But even so, there will still be times when we will be removed from places, careers or callings, people, and geographical residences through an invisible and loving source that knows more than we do, and many times sees what is coming before we can see it ourselves.

Conscious Choices

Raymond was at his wits end. When he arrived at The Helping Hand *that morning to prep for lunch, he found the kitchen in disarray. Dirty dishes were piled on the kitchen island, empty cartons of milk and plastic wrap were strewn about, and nothing was in its normal place. "There is no way I can be ready for the lunch crowd today Laura! The ingredients I was planning to use have evidently been EATEN, and with all the clean-up needed, I can't see how I will ever be able to catch up."*

Laura had spent the night with her grandmother the night before, arriving much later than usual that morning. Her grandmother was using her oxygen almost continually now, felt unusually weak, and Laura had

21

been forced to call the paramedics in order to calm her down. A call to the doctor had proved moot. He could only say, "I'm sorry. At this point, there is nothing more that we can do for her. Just let her rest comfortably, give her the anti-anxiety medication I prescribed, and hopefully she will sleep." Leaving Bernie to sleep by her grandmother's bedside, Laura had finally eased out late that morning to check in at The Helping Hand. She had called her only other existing relatives —two cousins who visited from time to time (always filling her grandmother's time by chatting non-stop about themselves), but they could not be bothered to adjust their plans and help her out.

"This isn't the first time this has happened," Raymond exclaimed while wiping down the counter. Turning toward Laura, he placed his hands on his hips, a wet towel in one hand, while the other hand seemed to be holding him down and steady, lest he lose whatever was left of his composure and personal space. "The residents at the shelter have been disregarding the guidelines. They come into the kitchen at all hours of the night and help themselves to anything they please. And Gary seems to be at the helm, orchestrating it all. I will be honest with you Laura. Things are not what they used to be. I have been thinking for a while now— my brother just opened a new restaurant on 7th Street—I'm going to have to start work there. Things have gotten too out of control here, and this boundary issue is the last straw. I'll be leaving at the first of next week."

Laura stayed at her grandmother's house again that night. Her parents had both died several years before, and with no other relatives except her two distant cousins, she and her grandmother were very close. For as long as she could remember, they had shared a very special bond. Like kindred spirits, Laura had lived a life that her grandmother had always dreamed about living herself. They went to places unspoken—places her grandmother never allowed others to enter or to know about. She had confided in Laura for many years, and Laura felt very protective of her.

Her greatest supporter and biggest fan, her grandmother had a deep and loving faith in her that knew no bounds. *"You are the most interesting person I have ever known,"* she would often say, and to Laura, this was the highest compliment she could ever remember receiving. Her grandmother knew who she was. She understood who she was. She accepted who she was. And she was in awe of her with a pride and love that swelled her heart. With her grandfather dying of a sudden stroke two years ago, her now small family had become more precious than ever before.

Packing up a few toiletries and Bernie's food, she felt compelled to move into the guestroom at the front of her grandmother's house. If her grandmother needed her during the night, she would be close by. Sleeping now in a small twin bed since her grandfather had died (*"I feel so lost now in that big bed!"* she had said), her grandmother often commented how safe, secure, and cozy she felt in her small intimate bedroom. When she first arrived at the house, Laura found her in her little bed, propped up by pillows, barefoot with knees pulled up against her chest like the school girl she had once been, looking as innocent and pure as a newborn. If it had not been for the oxygen tubes adding something very out of place to the picture, Laura would have wondered if this happy, carefree woman was actually in poor health at all.

They talked long into the night. *"You need to rest Grandma! I'm keeping you up far too long!"* Laura had begged. But her grandmother seemed suddenly tireless, strangely eager for Laura to know all things unsaid. Intimate stories to be passed along, to be sheltered and protected within a very new mind and heart, were being released into the heart of the night…free now to find their way to a very new steward, only to be released at another sacred time yet unknown. They talked about her grandfather; Laura listening with great interest as she heard a yet untold story surrounding their meeting and subsequent courtship. They had been married for nearly 60 years when he died, and the emptiness her grandmother felt *after his passing went rarely unnoticed. While gazing at a photo of him on her nightstand, her grandmother had gently fallen into a peaceful sleep.*

Feeling exhausted, Laura ventured into the bathroom for a hot shower. Her grandmother's bathroom always smelled of Ivory soap. With a familiar pale yellow fringe rug on the floor, surrounded by white walls, a white tile counter, and white towels, she often felt like she was intruding in a sacred space whenever she entered the bathroom. Betta, her grandmother's cleaning lady of 20 years, had kept it spotlessly clean, and it frequently looked untouched with a pristine and innocent feel, much like her grandmother looked tonight. Timeless, it had not changed for years, hovering in a strange time warp all its own. Laura dried off with a fresh towel smelling of her grandmother's favorite lilac. The sheer curtains on the window above her began to puff in and out… a gentle breeze had arrived, smoothing away the stresses of the day, and she was soon overcome by a need to sleep herself. This house had always been a calming balm for her— a place of reprieve, serenity, and security against the harshness of the outside world.

Laura was suddenly awakened by Bernie's wet nose nudging her shoulder. Illuminated in the darkness, the nightstand clock read 3:30. A neon green light blaring into the sweet space of sleep, it somehow felt out of place in this calm and familiar place. Nudge, nudge. Bernie was relentless. Laura had only seen Bernie this adamant about something one other time before. A few years ago, a candle had somehow caught her desk papers on fire, and Bernie had raced to find Laura, nudging her thigh until she finally relented, following him into her office. Just in time, as one moment later and the fire would have spread. Laura now knew to take Bernie's nudging seriously.

Following along behind him, he led her into her grandmother's room. Her nightstand lamp was still on, filling the room with a dim glow, but something felt strangely still and empty. "Grandma? Are you awake?"

Laura whispered. No answer. *"Grandma?"* As Laura moved in closer to the bed, she could see the soft outline of her grandmother's face resting gently on the pillow. Still facing her grandfather's picture, which was perched gently under the lamp, her eyes were closed, her nightgown a pale blue, a perfect match to her twinkly blue eyes, now softly flowing over her frail and bony shoulders. A sweet, contented, and serene smile, with the corners of her mouth tilted up ever so slightly, filled her still face.

"Grandma?" Laura tried again. Reaching out ever so gently, she took her grandmother's hand in hers. Cold and lifeless, it did not move. A cold chill filled Laura as her heart dropped. *"Oh Grandma..."* Laura moaned. *"Not yet. It's too soon!"* She searched her grandmother's face in vain for any kind of life or familiar movement, desperate for things to remain the same. Like an unwanted intruder, acceptance suddenly found its way to her, and she immediately went numb, turning her gaze toward the empty wall beyond.

She did not know how much time had passed, only that she was still in the same sitting position on her grandmother's bed—looking off into a sudden emptiness that had arrived on a swift horse out of nowhere, cutting through her world like a sharp sword in the dead of the night. Slowly coming back to this new and strange space where she now found herself—this empty, empty space—she laid her head upon her grandmother's chest and let the tears come in wracking sobs. A dam suddenly broke, releasing in a torrent of tears, all the stifled emotions she had held back for so long. Her greatest love, her soul companion, and her best friend, was forever gone. The special energy that Laura adored, in its own unique form called her grandmother, would never walk this earth again. A cord had broken, severing all things good and wonderful attached to her heart, with a sudden abandonment so deep, it left her with a hollow emptiness too new to understand. How in the world would she survive without her?

With the changes at the Helping Hand *and the sudden death of her grandmother, everything had suddenly broken wide open. A life of familiar comfort and predictability had finally reached its end. Over the past few months a bomb had exploded, bursting her world apart, and she could hold it together no longer. No more band-aids, supportive words, new additions, or rationalizations while waiting for things to come back to the familiar. Deep in her heart, she knew her life would never again be the same. Ever so slowly, it had melted away, disappeared, left her alone, pushed her out, and placed her in a no-man's land that she did not recognize nor understand.*

She thought she must be going mad now. She had to go—she had to get out—go somewhere else. She was turning inside out and upside down— her insides felt twisted and contorted. There was nothing left here in this strange, barren, and unfriendly place. She knew then that she must move on and leave it all behind. But where would she go?

. . .

So we now know, that as the planet continues its evolutionary process, there come pivotal times in each of our lives when we have now evolved out of our old roles and spaces and it is time to move on. Many times, we depart energetically, or rather at our mental and spiritual levels before we depart at our physical levels and with our physical bodies. When we depart, a vacuum is created, because even though we may still be there physically, the rest of us is not (the physical world is always the last to be affected). This newly created vacuum (whether in the physical reality, or simply at higher unseen levels) sends a trigger that a new space is now available. It is then filled with a lower vibrating energy, or one that now matches this space much better. So then, we have now moved on, even though at times our conscious minds may not yet have realized (or are willing to admit!) that this is what is now occurring. This is simply the law of metaphysics and how energy works and operates. In this way, the darker, denser, or lower vibrating energies always serve to push out the higher vibrating energies when it is time for the higher vibrating energies to move on. These mismatched energies can no longer exist in the same space. It is simply not possible. We move on no matter what, whether through conscious choice because we can no longer tolerate our old spaces and circumstances, or through a removal of our old selves and circumstances by a higher source from above.

Even though these laws of energy come into play at the lower levels of creation (thus, giving us the actual physical experience), there is also something at much higher levels occurring as well. These higher levels I will refer to as *soul levels* throughout the remainder of this book. Soul levels exist at the highest vibrational frequency, or rather in the invisible realms where everything was ultimately created, including our souls. At these levels, there is no right or wrong, no polarity, no darkness, but simply light and lots and lots of love. Light is all there is. In this way, there is never anything wrong either. Everything is always going in the same direction—which means everything is supporting the light in all ways as a perfect team. When our higher soul levels are dictating, we frequently have no actual conscious awareness of what we are doing and why. Things simply unfold in a perfect way with no intent or agenda at our conscious levels. But the more we evolve, the more we become connected to these higher soul levels within ourselves. And strangely enough, in the higher realms of reality (where we are all heading very rapidly now), there is never, but ever, any actual intent or agenda anyway…only love and states of simply *being*.

So then, many times an individual or a group of souls will come together at their higher soul levels and make another individual so miserable, or do something so atrocious, that the "wronged" individual will be forced to leave. This is a gift. These souls are supporting the individual in their process and with their journey and loving this individual enough to perform this service, even though they may not be conscious of why they are doing it. This higher soul level scenario also occurs when we are abruptly removed from the old—or rather when everything that no longer fits us abruptly leaves through seemingly no fault of our own (earth changes and catastrophic climatic events fit into this category as well). When we lose nearly *everything* all at once, we can know with certainty that we are indeed being primed for an arrival into a very new reality that is much, much better than the one we just left. We have simply outgrown all of the old and everything we created there, and now get to experience something that matches who we have now become in all ways. We have indeed "graduated," and the universe is now telling us that it is time for our next level of reality and experience. We are done—just like the old world we left behind, only most of the time we are done before the old world is done! And also know, that because things are being orchestrated at the highest level of reality and creation (or our soul levels), when we find ourselves in the challenging space of no space, or "the in-between," all our needs will be miraculously met as well.

This is a true death before a rebirth. The spiritual evolutionary process now occurring on the planet, or our ascension process as some call it, dictates that we literally die while we remain alive. In this way, we experience many of the same things a person does when they experience a physical death. We depart the earth plane and moves on into a much better experience in a very new space—only this time, we take our bodies with us. This is why we have to leave so much behind and let go of so much. People who die do not take their suitcases with them!

So then, how do we leave the old behind in a conscious way, through a deliberate choice?

Because of scenarios created by our spiritual evolutionary process, much like Laura, there are times along the way when we become acutely miserable in our current surroundings. We may no longer be able to tolerate certain individuals, jobs, geographical locations, systems, and the like. If we follow our own feelings, and allow ourselves to naturally gravitate to what feels good for us, we will willingly leave these now mismatched conditions and strive for something new and different that fits who and what we have now become.

Still, we may hold on for various reasons, whether we feel we need the security of the familiar, from a fear of a loss of identity, for financial reasons, from a sense of personal responsibility, or we may even be overly spiritually dedicated and cannot seem to discontinue our old roles. Whatever the case, when it is time to move on, it is time to move on, and if we do not consciously choose to leave the old behind, it will eventually be removed for us.

For Laura, her old world and old calling eventually becomes so miserable for her, and so shockingly intolerable, that she can take no more—which finally pushes her to get in her car and drive off, leaving it all behind. For Laura and for many of us, there are common themes that occur, which are lovingly pushing us out at our soul levels so that we will be motivated to move on:

- Our old spaces and prior callings are suddenly filled with disrespectful people.

- The people in our lives no longer "see" us. They either ignore us, or love to tell us about others in our line of work, or even who have helped them personally, whom they like much better. They see them, but no longer see us.

- Especially if we are loving or caring individuals— in a service related occupation, or even loving and caring to our friends and family—we are suddenly taken for granted, ignored, disrespected, put last, and it is expected that we will always "be there" no matter what. When this occurs, it is time to depart.

- We feel "insulted" in certain situations and with certain people.

- We feel deeply wounded and saddened when interacting with certain situations or certain people.

- Others feel they know more about our area of expertise than we do, and we are not revered.

- We are squeezed out by systems that make it impossible to provide the service we have provided in years prior, or we are unwilling to participate with how certain systems require us to interact.

- Our clients or individuals in our lives depend on us too much, hang on us, seemingly suck our energy dry, and will not stand on their own two feet.

- Generally speaking, as individuals and human beings, we are not "seen," acknowledged, revered, respected, and everything is about the other person or other entity.

When we can no longer tolerate the spaces where we have resided before, we have a conscious choice to depart. But where in the heck do we go? More about this further along...

Forced Departure

When I was in my mid-fifties, I purchased my first home. A large 5 bedroom home on over an acre of land, I bought it for reasons relating to my spiritual work and calling, or where I was at that time in my life. Up until then, I had moved frequently because my spiritual calling dictated it. It was now time for a very new phase to unfold for me, and this was an exciting time.

I would finally own my very own home! My entire life had been leading up to this moment, and a large house of my own fit in every way.

Being a simple person at heart, and resonating more deeply with quaint, old, and funky residences with lots of character and charm, I was never wildly passionate about the house itself. Everyone who entered the house marveled at its beauty, as it was new, quite large, very majestic, and had many extravagances. And everyone who entered the house was completely baffled by my ambivalent reaction to it as well. They thought I was crazy, that I would make it my own eventually, or even that I was simply acting weird. Who would not want a house such as this one? Nonetheless, I knew it would fit in with what was next in my life—with what I had dreamed about and felt deep within my soul for as long as I could remember. With a few tweaks and a bit of construction, I felt I could make it work. I needed a large home and grounds, as this space would be filled with lots of people one day.

Shortly after purchasing my home, much changed within the spiritual arena that I had called home for so long. After the dust settled and things sorted out at the higher levels of the spiritual evolutionary plan, everything had changed. I knew it was then time to connect to something new and different. In this way, my new house no longer fit with the new space I found myself in. By then, I had become comfortable there—and after all the years of many moves, and because it was my first permanent home, I decided to stay with it. I had been guided to this house and purchased it by a series of synchronistic miracles, had felt very protected and peaceful there, and felt I could make staying there work somehow. I could still use it, but now for a different purpose. WRONG!

My home had been owner financed, so in order to make it my own, it was time for me to remove myself from this situation. I had experienced a difficult time with the owner, as he was severely focused on himself, his own personal needs, very demanding, and making money was his primary focus. At higher levels, his purpose was to initially give me my home, and then it was planned that we part ways. With the new unheard of low interest rates then present, I began the process of keeping this space by applying for a home refinance. Even though I had not generated any money for several months (as I had discontinued my prior work due to the changes in the spiritual arena), miracles had always occurred for me. I was also encouraged by others to give it a try. The bank was even open to the possibility. Wanting deeply to hold onto my house, I told myself that if the refinance did not go through, I would sell it. This would be my indication and a sign that I should sell. I quite honestly could not imagine selling my house. It was very far out of my frame of any kind of possibility— I absolutely could not imagine it in my wildest dreams. Over time, this house had become my very personal space. I had lived in the southwest for many years; this had always been the area where I resonated most, and now I owned a home here. But in addition, the energies on the planet and the universal plan had gone through a series of twists and turns, and it was still not clear whether staying here would be in my best interest or not. At some times, it was clear that I should stay and how this would be in alignment with the new possibilities for the planet, and at other times the energies and souls on the planet were still trying to make up their minds as to how things were going to unfold.

Even though everything looked good, because I had not worked for several months, the refinance did not go through. Ignoring what I had declared as "a sign," I decided to try with another bank. I simply could not move on again. I had let go and lost so much up until that point, that I had a deep desire for some kind of anchor and familiarity until I was up and going again with something new. I was not ready to let go of my personal space from which my own creations stemmed. This had been a great space for me for over a year—the most private and peaceful living space I had encountered yet in my life. I was quite honestly surprised that the refinance did not go through, as I had been gifted this house and felt I would eventually make it mine in an effortless way. So my bullheaded nature decided to contact a new bank the following day. But before I could, I was stopped in my tracks.

The very next morning, I awoke to a bulldozer outside my bedroom window—a house was being built by the individual who had owner financed my home—and the house was for him. He would be my new neighbor! As the day progressed, the beautiful lot next door—which I had planned on purchasing one day to create a garden sanctuary for the nature spirits and wildlife—was being ravaged by tractors, torn up, and replaced by the energy of a money machine. My massive view of the mountains was being blocked as well, my bird sanctuary torn up—all because a new house was literally going up only a few feet from my own. As I looked out my massive floor to ceiling windows, all I could see now was the new construction of his house. My intended new space for future higher level creations was now going to be occupied by anything but. Well, okay... it was unquestionably time to move on.

Although I was never able to interact at physical levels with the man who financed my home and who was moving next door (as he did not understand communication, courtesy, unity and working as a team), in time, I grew to love his soul, as I was ever so grateful he had forced me to move on. If not for him, I would never have found myself in a new and magical space, filled with everything I had ever wanted, and with everything that fit me oh so much better. At our higher soul levels, we had indeed loved and helped each other, and were on the same team.

The very day that the bulldozer arrived, I contacted a real estate agent and put my home up for sale. My agent hired stagers to come and work with the contents of my home in order to make it look as appealing as possible to prospective buyers. I had a mystical/nature décor, so there was a lot to be done, and according to my agent, it would really make a difference. His normal stager was not available, so he found a new substitute that could come right away, as there was a real estate tour scheduled in a few short days. In the meantime, I de-cluttered and packed up all of my knick-knacks, thus removing most of the nature/mystical/ancient energy that I so resonated with my entire life. I willingly did this, as I knew that the house needed to be seen—not me, but the house. I needed to be invisible, gone, and my essence undetectable, thus allowing for the house itself to resonate with whoever chose to purchase it, making the likelihood of selling as great as possible.

The substitute stagers arrived shortly thereafter. All I can say is *ouch!* Very aggressive, they threw carpets out the door, told me to remove my toothbrush from the house ("Don't even leave it in the drawer!"), took comforting photos of my grandchildren and my life, and anything and everything that was *me*, out of the house. It had to look like no one really lived there, and at invisible energetic levels, no one did! "These stagers are much more aggressive than my normal stagers," my real estate agent said. "You don't say!" I could only think to myself. Feeling violated, attacked, and disrespected, I felt as if a tornado had arrived and blown out my old self in one brief afternoon! But at the highest soul levels, the stagers were lovingly supporting me in the final stages of leaving my old self behind. I would never have wiped myself this clean on my own—I would have never felt a need to erase so much—if it were not for these two special women.

At first, it was difficult living in a house that was not an expression of *me*. I was no longer in a comfort zone of familiarity. The connection to myself then, was also gone, as well as my connection to everyone and everything else in recent months—even my work which had been my calling, not just a regular old job, was gone as well. And now, I did not even have the nature spirits outside my window to connect to! After a few days and weeks of having nothing of my old self to connect to, I looked in the mirror one day and noticed my signature necklace. Handmade by a Hopi Elder, it was made of sterling silver and depicted an image of emergence that had been my identity for a very long time. He had personally placed it around my neck. Suddenly, I could not relate to it anymore. It was no longer *me*. Depicting an image that had been my purpose on this earth for my entire life, I removed it from my neck, as it no longer fit who I had now become. At this point, it felt like the most natural and comforting thing to do.

Now knowing that my home was soon to depart, I began to ponder about where to live next. I had lived in and resonated with the Southwest for many years, so out of habit and very naturally, I began to explore other areas there that might fit my needs. Absolutely nothing felt right. Soon the realization hit that I would be letting go of the Southwest as well. And along with this realization came another one— I could not fit all my belongings into a moving truck. I would need to sell most of my furniture and many of my personal items. I had sold my belongings before a move in times past, but this felt very different. Wanting to hold on to *anything*, as so much had been removed in recent times, it soon became evident that I was not yet done with the massive cleansing that seemed to have a mind of its own.

At that point, I had recently left my calling and prior work, my father had died a few months before, several other friends and prior intimate partners had suddenly died (physically and literally), and with the exception of my daughter and grandchildren, I had become estranged from all my relatives within the past few months as well. And now my personal identity was being removed, leaving nothing much for me to connect to. I was being wiped clean. *Going, going... gone.* And there was nothing, but nothing on the horizon for me to connect to.

For me, being forced out still had certain elements of choice. I have always felt most comfortable being in alignment with what is occurring in my life, so I usually willingly go along with what feels the best and where I feel the best. Being forced out or encouraged to move on then, can have an array of variance in severity, all dependent upon how in touch with our own divine selves we may be. Choosing to sever connections and move toward spaces that feel good, offers us more of an experience involving choice and personal power. Evidently, I was not yet ready to "die" completely (or so I thought), so the universe gave me a big nudge. There are also more severe ways of being forced out through no fault of our own. For example: Losing a job through a layoff or firing, having a spouse suddenly ask for a divorce, having a house burn down, having our computer totally crash with all aspects of our lives and work within it, having our grown children refuse to speak to us, and the like. When it is hard to let go, it will be done for us. And as strange as it may sound, *we are always, but always, better off without what we have lost.*

The Loss of Our Loved Ones

Losing our loved ones (human as well as animal companions) is perhaps one of the most difficult aspects of experiencing a re-birth. It can be heart wrenching and heartbreaking at the depths of our being—making us wonder if we will indeed be able to survive this challenging and ever testing spiritual evolutionary process.

Because we lose what no longer fits us, we can lose our loved ones in basically two ways, but either way, this can still be a very difficult and painful experience: Our loved ones can either depart 1) through the physical death process, or 2) through estrangement.

The Physical Death…Leaving the Body Behind

There were several possible scenarios for the End Times. Originally, the spiritual evolutionary plan was created with the least possible challenges and suffering, so that a natural and smooth transition could occur. But with all things on the earth, the souls who reside here and the choices they make are what will dictate, as free will is a mandatory requirement of the makings of the spiritual evolutionary process and of existence on the earth.

So in this way, the plan for the End Times had many twists and turns, and within these twists and turns were times of great darkness and suffering. Each and every soul had opportunities to grow and change—to become what they had originally planned on becoming—embodying their true and authentic selves. But many souls instead chose to hold on tightly to their old ways, or to what they believed was best for their own personal interests or whom they believed themselves to be. Fear took over along with the adamant holding on to the old or to a warped and lost version of a vision held by many, and thus, darkness ensued.

Because of this situation, some souls decided to depart earlier than they had originally planned. Each of us at our soul levels has a choice to die via a physical death and end our current experience here at certain windows of opportunity, or pre-planned "exit points." We can depart at any of these exit points or pass them up and wait for the next one. So then, when the train stops at our current place of residence, we can get on board or we can wave it on by, turning then from the train depot where we suddenly find ourselves, and returning to our place of residence for yet more of the earth experience. But know as well, that because we are in the End Times, these exit points are very numerous now.

When Henry was in his late 70's, he had a heart attack, died, and was revived and brought back. For his remaining few years until his imminent death of cancer, he searched for the reason he had been brought back, but he never consciously found it. At his higher soul levels, he came back after his heart attack in order to have a different experience with his life. His soul knew that the earth was about to discontinue all it had ever been, and he wanted one last shot at having a human experience here before things would change forever more. His heart attack was his wake-up call and his trigger for creating a very different life, if even for a very short while. Eventually, he decided to depart with certainty, as he had experienced everything he could and there was nothing more left for him and nowhere left to go. The second time he chose to depart via cancer, as a lingering and longer death process would enable him to make sure that those around him were taken care of before he departed. He also left at this time because he wanted to leave while his dignity was still intact—things had begun to rapidly unravel in his life and he did not wish to stay during the transition from the old world to the new world.

This type of scenario is what is occurring now on the planet for all of us. If we choose to stay after our "death while still alive" experience, we will then go on to a very new experience on the earth and start over with a very clean slate. And this is why we have to leave *nearly everything* behind. Although Henry wanted a last shot at a very new experience, he was not in a position to experience this, nor willing to leave everything behind. If we do not leave nearly everything behind, we will only re-create much of the same, only perhaps with a different twist, thus believing that we are starting over with a very new existence, when in truth, we are not. So in this way, he eventually did have his intended experience, but he ultimately chose to leave his body behind in order to do it.

When it is time for our loved ones to depart through a physical death, for whatever reason they have chosen, they will indeed depart. For some, they feel as if there is nowhere left to go that fits what they think their experience here should look like, or what they feel the world is all about. And yet for others, they are unable to move through a pain so deep (or rather an emotional wound), see no way to do or be something different, and choose to depart. For those in loving relationships who suddenly lose a partner, for instance, there is yet another reason our loved ones die. They want us to have a new and different experience while there is still time, and thus die so that we will now be free to find and cultivate a new self — a self that many times closely resembles aspects of the partner or loved one who departed. Frequently, in long standing relationships, partners balance themselves out. So in this way, a wife for instance, may be left behind by a husband of many years, so that she can now have a very new experience during the final days of the old earth, while she now takes on the attributes her husband used to own. She will now get to do things differently. Her loving husband has intentionally left her, in order to give her this valuable opportunity. We all have the choice at our soul levels to stay here for the End Times or to depart. In this regard, living and dying will occur in epidemic proportions in times to come. There are many now, who are having their very last experiences with the old world, or old earth, before it ceases to exist. This is their last shot before everything changes forever more. For whatever reason, they did not have this opportunity before. They are being given the chance to take it now.

Losing our beloved animal companions can be a heart wrenching experience as well. When our animal companions no longer fit with what surrounds them on the planet, or have endured enough, they choose to depart. At times as well, they will take on the emotional pain of their owners, act like a sponge or buffer, and contract cancer or disease and depart in this way. Either way, they almost always return to us in a new and different animal form, and this new form is rejuvenated and now fits in with the next leg of our journey. Even so, many of us receive so much love and companionship from our animal families, that losing them can be as devastating, or at times even more devastating, than losing a human family member.

Because the End Times are so unique, run deep, high, and wide, and are occurring when changes are rampant and imminent at our deepest soul levels, departing souls are a very normal part of this experience. In this way, each and every one of us can very easily depart through physical death at any given moment. I have been given this choice in recent months more times than I choose to count! We are not anchored here like we used to be. Staying here now is entirely up to us when each now frequent exit point arrives.

Death Through Estrangement…Leaving Our Loved Ones Behind
Losing our loved ones through estrangement can not only be heartbreaking, but can be acutely confusing as well, leaving us bewildered, shocked, and wounded deep within our hearts.

But even so, when we lose our loved ones through estrangement, in time we somehow go numb in that area of connection, and are strangely protected through a loss of feeling and pain that we might normally experience. And just as strangely, we most always feel a sense of great relief, as the problems and dramas of those we leave behind no longer fit with where we now find ourselves.

The same process or scenario holds true for estrangement as for most everything with the spiritual evolutionary process. If any of our loved ones are not vibrating at our level, or are not at our level of spiritual evolution, we will experience a disconnect. Remember, higher and lower vibrating energies cannot exist in the same space for very long. But even more important, or rather the true reason we experience the disconnect, is because at our soul levels, our loved ones who have not reached our own spiritual levels, are encouraging us to move on, as they are still lingering behind and have yet more to complete. So in this way, these disconnects come from a very loving place, as all souls are acting in unity at their soul levels.

(In times past, there were souls on the planet who came (or were born) during this particular time in order to assist with the evolutionary plan of the birth of a new world or reality. These souls gave it their all, and were eventually released when they had done all they could possibly do (kindly refer to the metaphysical section in *Chapter 1* for greater detail.) These souls transmuted enormous amounts of lower vibrating energy through themselves, and in addition, assisted other souls on the planet with this process as well. This time is now over. These souls can do no more. So in this way, if any of their loved ones have now been left behind, these more evolved souls are no longer required (according to their soul plans) to assist them, or anyone else on the planet for that matter.)

If there is a strong heart connection, experiencing a disconnect from our loved ones can be very painful when it initially occurs. And even more painful, can be the confusion and bewilderment that accompanies these disconnects. If one member of a prior relationship is not willing to disconnect, then the other member will do it for them. For the remaining member, or rather the one left holding on, this can be confusing and painful. But remember—at our soul levels, we are always, but always, assisting each other and going in the same direction. There is great love at these levels, and through this love, we are always helping each other.

In what ways do these disconnects occur, and how can we identify them?

- A friend or loved one will somehow never be available when we are. We will miss their calls, they will forget to call us back, or vice versa, and we are somehow never able to come together.

- They will consciously avoid us or we will avoid them.

- Their lives will be about nothing that remotely interests us, and vice versa.

- We will find that we no longer enjoy the conversations we have had in the past.

- Their thinking or beliefs make absolutely no sense to us.

- When we are around them, we feel invisible, disrespected, taken for granted, and not "seen."

- Our loved ones from the past suddenly begin acting strangely, make no sense, seem lost in a place we cannot relate to or understand, and leave us perpetually bewildered.

- We feel turned upside down, spun around, traumatized, and thrown off balance when we are around them.

- We are treated very badly by those we love, and most times feel "insulted" or treated like we are grossly insignificant.

- Our love, support, and caring is "expected" and almost demanded by them, while all their attention goes to other people and places.

- They feel they know more than we do, and that we are the ones with "a problem."

- Our loved ones view us as weak and overly sensitive.

At our higher soul levels, a very different scenario is occurring, and this scenario is comprised of the purest love between two souls, even though what is occurring at the lower levels of experience may seem to dictate otherwise.

For whatever reason distinct to each soul, some souls have chosen to lag behind, and in this way, they force their loved ones to move forward so that their loved ones can experience heaven on Earth in every way. Some souls have not finished completing what they came to do, and must complete their plans before they can move on. Other souls have chosen to stay behind and assist other loved ones who are lost. And yet other souls still have healing to do, as they have not yet finished what they came to transmute or accomplish in their first experience here. These souls cannot go where more evolved souls now reside. They have not yet "earned" their new residency, and so they create very bizarre, confusing, and disrespectful behavior in order to force a more evolved soul to move ahead and out of their space.

Initially, we can all choose to move ahead with more ease before the more "radical" behavior begins in these relationships. But if we choose to hold on, these relationships will become so uncomfortable for us, that we have no choice but to sever them. The souls who are asking us to disconnect from them may many times leave us scratching our heads, saying "What the....?", or even "Have you lost your mind????!!!!" At this point, we cannot remotely understand their actions or thought processes (nor can they understand ours), as they do not come from a more evolved interaction or behavior that exists in the higher levels of reality. Pure love is a straight and simple shot—anything else has twists, turns, manipulations, controlling behaviors, or gross self-absorptions that come from the lower levels of reality.

At the lower levels of reality, many souls have become lost for the same reason: They have become entwined in their ego selves and with what they believe their reality should look like. They have become lost in their own world with seemingly no awareness that anything exists other than themselves and their own personal needs. Being perpetually lost in one's self is simply an indication of a disconnect from the new world or heaven on Earth that is now available to others. So in this way, being disconnected from heaven on Earth, or the new world, means a disconnect as well to those who are now residing there, or at least about to reside there.

In the more evolved levels of reality, souls always come together in unity and equality. This means that each soul sees, acknowledges, and highly reveres all other souls, including his/herself. Each soul has specific gifts and talents that they emit very naturally, and these gifts, or essences of each soul, are widely seen and acknowledged by others. In this way, there is always equal give and take from one soul to another (giving is actually not the best word here, as these soul essences simply exist in a state of being, and are then utilized by the whole when needed). Having this equal exchange and utilization of energy occurring between souls, creates a grid or level of energy that enables a reality to exist and sustain itself. This is also what creates a shift in consciousness, or a leap in human evolution, when enough souls reach this point of living and being.

This is specifically what *did not* occur during the years 2008, 2009, and 2010. Each soul has something specific to offer that serves to create a whole, and these essences need to be acknowledged in order to be sustained. It was planned that the souls on the planet would come together in unity, and begin the creation of the new world through this higher level grid of connection between souls. Unfortunately, the majority of the souls on the planet could only see themselves.

The separations then, between our loved ones and ourselves, usually occurs when this unity consciousness is not present between souls, and especially if there is no love. When one soul cannot see outside of him/herself, and revere and connect through love with another soul, the grid then, cannot exist. And even if one soul greatly loves another with a true and pure love, the recipient of this love cannot accept and embody it until they have evolved sufficiently and are able to return it in kind. The love simply acts as a mirror, reflecting whom these souls currently believe themselves to be, and if they are not ready to look within themselves and make change, they will not like what they see and disconnect. Other lost souls will willingly continue to accept love from another soul, as they easily take it from the outside but do not give it in return as it does not yet exist within them, forcing a disconnect then, from the soul giving the love. Either way, these disconnects occur between evolved souls and their lost loved ones no matter what the individual circumstances.

The planet is attempting to propagate love, as in the more highly evolved realities, this is the glue that holds everything together. In times past, more highly evolved souls on the planet embodied a great sense of "mission" and purpose, as it was greatly needed at that time to get the ball rolling. It is now time for the heart energy to take the greatest precedence. So in this way, if a soul is still stuck in the never-ending wheel of their first designated purpose, and has forgotten about unity and love, they become lost within themselves. Unity and love is the air we breathe in the new world. It is our atmosphere and our grid—it is what will hold everything together. And yes, we will each have a specific purpose, role, or personal essence, but until enough love is propagated, these roles and purposes will have nowhere to reside.

Ben was born with a gift for making money. He also felt it his duty and responsibility to hire others to help him with his projects, and in this way, he viewed others as under his domain, feeling that he was "helping" them in some way, even though it was always *his* way. One of his projects involved a substantial loan to Susan. Susan had recently lost her job, but told Ben not to worry, as she felt she had enough in her savings that she could cover the loan for a while longer. She made it very clear to Ben that she was stressed about living off what was left of her savings until she found another job. One day soon after, Ben knocked on her door. He proceeded to ask Susan if she could please pay off the loan now, as he felt it would benefit her by saving her interest. Susan could only be left scratching her head in confusion. Later it became clear to her that because Ben was highly focused on his gift of making money and in investing, he was only able to see the fact that Susan had ready cash available and that he could use it to benefit himself. He could only see things relating to money and interest. He was not able to see Susan herself in any way, and certainly unable to see her situation. All he could see was himself and money. Ben was lost in the merry-go-round of his own ego and purpose, and what he believed the world to be about. He was stuck in a box of his own making—a box without love and unity.

Louise was a successful business owner with a web site that generated massive amounts of traffic. Louise and Terry had been great friends for many years. As Terry began to pull together the makings of her own passion and bring it into a business model, Louise offered to put a blurb about Terry on her website—just to get her started with some exposure. Terry immediately generated enough business for an entire year. At first, Terry was very grateful to Louise, but very soon, Terry began to get caught up in her own reality and lost in herself. She began telling her clients that she thought Louise had some very strange ideas and that her own were much, much better. She was rarely available to talk to Louise, and would even refuse to answer her phone if she saw it was Louise calling, although Louise rarely called her. Even so, every week, Terry would continue to call Louise and ask her for advice, even though she told others that Louise was very wrong in her way of viewing the world. Terry loved Louise's loving and caring energy. Eventually, Louise began to feel very insignificant when talking to Terry on the phone, and in addition, what Terry said and how she led her life made absolutely no sense to Louise. She continually hung up the phone after each conversation feeling bewildered and confused. Louise was no longer enjoying their conversations. Terry was unable to see outside of herself and how she viewed the world. She was not able to see that Louise had beliefs that fit in perfectly with her own, and that her beliefs were a very important part of Louise's beliefs. Terry could only see her own agenda, and had become lost in thinking that it was the only one. She had forgotten about the whole, was using Louise to get love and caring, and was unable to work as a team.

At their higher soul levels, Ben was encouraging Susan to disconnect from their relationship, as it no longer fit where she was heading. Terry needed to disconnect from Louise, as Terry was greatly needed in the mainstream—where her soul had always intended she belong. She needed to discontinue hanging onto Louise for her source of love and support, as she would be offering this herself to others at the mainstream level.

But what if circumstances are dictating that we continue to interact with lower level energies before we can disconnect? As always, things are being orchestrated at the higher levels of reality, so in this way, we are always being loved, protected, and taken care of. While we are in the midst of disconnecting and still forced to interact with lower level entities, because they are almost always caught in their hamster wheel of self-containment and of what they believe their world to be about, they frequently cut their own throats. What this means is that even though they believe they are "winning" by staying true to their beliefs and themselves, their actions frequently serve to benefit a more highly evolved soul during the disconnect process. Love always wins, if even through an interaction with a lost soul.

So through this amazing and rare experience of spiritual evolution, in order to arrive in a very new world and reality of our making, we experience massive and painful loss. We lose loved ones, jobs, careers, homes, personal property, and perhaps most severely, our own identity.

The Loss of Our Identity

When my father died, I remember feeling that I was no longer a daughter. I had been a daughter for 55 years, and was a daughter no more. When I eventually lost my own daughter, I remember feeling that I was now no longer a mother. And when the remainder of my family was lost as well, I realized that I was now no longer a sister, aunt, or cousin. When the spiritual evolutionary plan that I had been a part of my entire life also ended (or rather abruptly changed), and my proposed part in it ended, I remember feeling that I no longer had a purpose here—or at least one I had come to embody my entire life. And as I had experienced so much stress in 2010, leaving me feeling aged beyond my years, when I now looked in the mirror, I had no idea whose face was looking back at me.

With so much stripped away and removed, we eventually reach a threshold where we are no longer the person we used to be, and are no longer living the life we used to live. Our purpose then, dramatically changes, along with how we used to fit into the old reality. In the end, we find ourselves with a new purpose and a new "normal." And this new normal has a very specific intention— to be completely centered around love, with a reverence and gratitude for anything and everything in existence.

If our connections to biological family, or blood ties, are not centered around love (from both parties), they will then undergo a disconnect. So in this way, blood ties no longer have the meaning that they had in the past. These old identities, or how we interacted in our biological families, then cease to exist. In the end, love creates the only connection, and it no longer matters with whom.

When we lose our careers, residences, loved ones, and much else that no longer fits us, we end up with a substantial loss of ego as well. We may no longer know who we are and what we are doing here on the earth. And with others out there seemingly ignoring us, as we are unable to be "seen" by those who reside at lower levels of existence, this spiritual evolutionary process can become quite challenging indeed!

With the loss of so much of our old identity, how do we know what to do or be next? And how do we now find our way? Before we find ourselves in very new spaces, with new identities and ways of being, we must first experience "the in-between."

3

NO SENSE OF PLACE... "THE IN-BETWEEN"

BEFORE WE ARRIVE IN VERY new spaces with very new connections that fit us oh so much better, we go through the challenging phase of "the in-between"— where we are neither here nor there. Similar to menopause where we are too old to be young and too young to be old, we no longer fit within the lives we left behind, and our new lives have not yet arrived. This space of no space, where we dangle with no foundation to stand upon and nothing yet to hold onto, can make us feel as if we are floundering in mid-air, while we wait for the process of all the disconnects to complete. This can be one of the most difficult aspects of the death of the old.

As human beings, we very naturally crave a sense of belonging...a place where we fit in, feel comfortable, know who we are, and what is ours to do and be. At times, we may find ourselves alone and isolated while experiencing "the in-between," creating feelings of loneliness, invisibility, lack of value and worth, and at best, confusion and insecurity as we have nothing much to connect to.

When we are neither here nor there, our lives are basically gone. As if in a coma, we are now in a strange space that has no remote connection to anything currently occurring on the planet. We may wonder how in the world we will ever survive financially, how anyone can possibly help us when we have been removed from so much, and we may even wonder deep down if we are now destined to depart this planet forever…perhaps preparing to contract some fatal disease and soon die altogether.

One of the most challenging aspects of "the in-between" is the intense feelings of departure it creates, making us feel as if we can leave this world at any given moment. Because we have been removed from so much and are experiencing strong feelings of disconnection, we can get a very distinct feeling that our "time is up." And when there is nothing left for us here, and we may feel that there is nowhere remotely left for us to go, we may find ourselves thinking "What's the point? There is nothing here for me. I am no longer needed. There is nothing holding me here. It must be time for me to die as my life is over. I am done."

We are indeed preparing to die, but it is only the death of our old selves before we arrive in a very new world—the new world that has been destined to arrive for eons of time. So in this way, we may feel very certain that death is an imminent event for us and on the very near horizon, when in fact what we are really feeling is the loss of a self that existed in the old world—a world where we no longer belong. In essence, we are dying and being reincarnated once again, but this time, we will be re-born as a new and much more highly evolved human being, as we need to match the energy of the new world.

Along with the obvious, "the in-between" has other characteristics that are fairly common and worth mentioning, as they can create confusion and at times be frightening. In addition, a handful of these characteristics resemble Alzheimer's disease, and for very good reason. In the old world, when it was time for a soul to depart and this soul found it difficult to leave, many times he/she would get Alzheimer's disease. Some souls were very attached to a soul mate or other loved ones, and did not want to leave them behind. Some souls could no longer tolerate this world, and so they departed via Alzheimer's. And yet others had varied reasons for wanting to stay here longer than intended, so they stayed "half-way." No matter what the reason, Alzheimer's disease leaves a soul in an in-between state for a lengthy period of time. They are slowly easing themselves out of this reality. They may not want to be here, but they do not want to depart either. In this way, they are neither here nor there. Because these souls will not allow themselves to depart entirely, they spend intermittent amounts of time here, and intermittent amounts of time stuck in "the in-between." When in "the in-between" during the ascension process, it is of a much shorter duration and certainly much easier to navigate through and function within, than when literally contracting Alzheimer's. But nonetheless, the symptoms are remarkably similar, as when in this space, we are neither here nor there. And of course, Alzheimer's is a devastating blow to families and a very challenging situation, with ramifications that do not remotely compare to the temporary resemblances that the "in be-between" mimics. Below are the most common symptoms of being in "the in-between"— and remember, they do not last forever:

- *An acute feeling of vulnerability.* Because we are neither here nor there, with nothing to hold onto and no attachments, we are dangling in mid-air. In this space, we are unable to enmesh ourselves within anything, which leaves us out in the open for anyone or anything to have their way with us. We have no anchor and no walls around us. This is the time when we will usually experience abuses from darker energies. Because we are in essence "homeless," we are now more subject to these darker or denser energies and can feel very vulnerable. As we move into our new spaces more securely, through the process of letting go, we will eventually cease to have these unpleasant experiences and a new power and security will eventually find us.

- *An all-encompassing lack of self-confidence.* We have lost our old selves. We are no longer who we used to be, and our new selves have not yet arrived. Add to this a disrespect from others and feelings of being invisible, and it is no wonder that many times we find ourselves feeling lost, "less than," and unsure of much of anything. In addition, this process also prohibits us from moving forward, so in this way, we may feel a severe lack of control as well. And being that we are unable to manifest anything whatsoever during this stage (because our subconscious higher soul selves are what is molding and controlling), our lack of control can be all-encompassing. Our physical, or conscious selves, are no longer at the helm.

- *We forget where we are.* We can be driving down the road, and suddenly forget where we are, where we were going, what day it is, and even who we are. We can go into a room and forget why we are there, or we can go to a store and forget what we came for, let alone where we parked our car! We can wake up in the morning, and even though we are in our bedrooms, we don't know where we are. When we are in "the in-between," we are neither here nor there, and in this way, when in transit, we can easily become lost. While driving, if we simply just relax our minds for a minute, our current reality will catch up very shortly and we will then be back in alignment with where we are.

- *We are unable to finish a sentence or remember the names of things.* Similar to the reasons above, only this occurs while talking. We are preparing to begin anew, so this means that everything will soon have a new and different meaning. Our interpretations from the past will soon be replaced by new and more elevated perceptions, so meanings then cease to exist. We can be in mid-sentence and completely forget the names and labels of objects, people, or places. In regard to finishing a sentence, we have simply lost our place, as we are neither here nor there, and unable then, to connect to anything. We begin, get so far, and then get lost as there is nothing yet up ahead to grab onto. And during other stages of the removal of the old, we may feel stunned, in a funk, and be unable to talk at all! Most of these symptoms ease as we eventually progress forward.

- *We feel very old and worn out...as if we have aged 100 years in the past few.* Well, what can I say? Our old lives are over, so we feel used up, ravaged, depleted, exhausted, and just plain worn out — all that is left of our old selves has been utilized far beyond what was intended. Our old selves are indeed at the end of their time here. After we are born again, we are infused with a new life force resembling the new world or new reality, and our old shells are then put to bed so to speak. We do indeed become rejuvenated—I can attest!—and our energy returns in droves. We look younger and more vibrant as well.

- *We find ourselves having our own "life review" as we examine our prior life on a regular basis.* We are done with our old lives and our old selves, and done with old relationships and old jobs, and done with old residences, and done with our prior spiritual calling, and done with...with...with...it all. In this way, we may find ourselves reviewing it all, processing it, making sense of what it was all about, and so forth. These are simply symptoms of letting go before we move on into the new, where all these things will be replaced by things that we have never experienced before. And these new things will be much better.

- *At times, we may feel as if we are sinking into a deep hole with nothing to pull us up.* We are bottoming out and dropping down as low as we can get, as there is nothing yet to hold onto to keep us elevated at a reasonable level. We may feel that we are falling, falling, falling. It can be dark down there! We may get stuck at the bottom, then find a few things to grab onto. Thinking we are finally on our way up, they suddenly fall away and we are nowhere once again. These strange "drops" do not last forever, and cease to exist altogether when our new lives eventually become intact.

- *Insomnia.* Subconsciously, we are afraid to let go, as we do not know where we will end up. The new shore has not yet arrived, and we may find ourselves jerking awake as we attempt to drift off, perhaps fearful that the cords holding us to the earth are no longer doing their job. Similar to feelings of vulnerability, as we are no longer here nor there, but homeless and unprotected, bouts of insomnia become most intense immediately preceding an arrival into a new space. It can be hard to sleep on the commuter train! Once we arrive in our very new spaces, we will once again sleep like babies. At other times, we stay awake as things are not yet ready in the new space—even in dreamtime! We cannot go where the construction crews are busily building the new.

- *An inability to write a sentence, formulate a complete thought, grasp a concept, or concentrate.* We might have a thought and then suddenly it completely leaves our consciousness and for all our efforts, we cannot find it again. We may be required to review legal documents, and find we need to utilize every modicum of pure concentration to focus and comprehend what we are reading. We may try and write a letter or compose other works, and struggle at length to write anything that remotely makes sense. We may find that we completed some kind of paperwork days before, and do not even remember doing it! Our thinking is foggy and we are seemingly brain dead with mush for brains. Emotions, on the other hand, seem to remain intact, as *feeling* is essentially a higher way of navigating in our new spaces. Nonetheless, as we progress through the birth canal, our brains eventually return to a more palpable operating capacity as they align with our new way of being and with what we will soon be doing.

- *General memory loss.* At times, we may find that we cannot remember what happened the day before or even a few moments before. And we may tell others the same stories again and again, forgetting that we had already given them the same information. Short-term memory loss occurs when we are in transit during this process and long-term memory loss occurs because we are leaving our prior lives behind. They may seem like they are now at the end of a long, dark tunnel somewhere far, far away.

- *Hot flashes and night sweats.* Our spiritual evolutionary process mimics menopause in nearly every way. Both men and women experience these common symptoms. Hot flashes are most prevalent when releasing and burning off old energy, and also the energy of the ego. (More on this further along.)

- *All in all, we may feel as if we are not all here.* We may feel that we are not as alert or sharp as we normally are, that we are not on top of things, that we do not know the answers to things anymore, that we are behind the times, or even that we are not on top of our game like we used to be. These particular feelings can last a few years if we are in spaces where we have been waiting for others to catch up. We are experiencing symptoms of having our souls move on into a space that has yet to be created, while what is left of our old selves is still in the old. We have evolved out of our old spaces, but are still physically there. In this way, we may feel as though we are not all here.

- *Heat stroke.* Similar to hot flashes and night sweats, heat stroke is common when in transition or when the planet is detoxing as a whole. In this way, our animal companions can experience heat stroke as well. We can have heat stroke in the dead of a cold winter. Staying hydrated is vitally important during these times as is staying as quiet as possible. Heat stroke results from a burning off of old energy as higher energies bombard the planet during specific times.

When we are living in "the in-between," we are prohibited from moving forward. At our higher soul levels, we are indeed at the helm of our lives, even though we may feel helpless and lost at our conscious levels. What this means is that we may attempt to move forward, create something new, go outside of our "box" of staying put, and be completely blocked from doing so. Nothing, but nothing will be in alignment with the spaces we are currently inhabiting because... we are in the space of no space. We are nowhere. We will be unable to find anything that fits, no matter what arena of our lives we are attempting to add to.

While occupying this space of no space in seeming suspended animation, at the higher levels of our spiritual evolutionary process, we are being molded into a very new person—pushed and shoved, held back, and redefined before we move forward. We must—absolutely must—fit these new spaces before we are able to occupy them. Energies, then, from high above are navigating things for us. So even though we may feel helpless at times, with a gross lack of confidence and power, there are powers far beyond our own conscious selves that are perfectly navigating our course for us. All we need do then, is get out of the way and be still. If we are stubborn by nature and refuse to comply with these loving powers that are here to assist us, as perhaps we like doing things on our own, and *even if* we are somehow able to create anything during this time (which is highly unlikely), we will only have to undo what we have created in times to come. If we attempt to move into any new creations we formulated while in "the in-between," when we are finally released, they will not remotely fit where we now belong and it will become immediately evident that we wasted our prior time, energy, and at times, finances as well. Being blocked then, or held back, only serves to help and assist us in the long run. So even though at times we may feel as if we are in prison, this is a time as well, when patience and trust can be great virtues. As we begin to move forward in slow and steady increments, frequently we find that we can now create, but only *half* of things. This means that one part is just what we desire or need, but not *all.* Absolutely nothing, then, fits just right in all ways.

At one point when I was personally experiencing this remolding process, it became very clear to me that I was being held hostage, or what I came to refer to as "being in protective custody" before I could move forward once again. My large home became my only world, because if ever I ventured out, I would be met with a massive wall of un-productivity.

Absolutely nothing would move forward or complete, and each and every one of the few items I purchased during that time had to be returned for various reasons. I soon came to accept that I was in a strange protective custody that felt safe and secure, even though I was not generating any income during that time and even though nothing new was seemingly ready to arrive for me. At one point, I simply had to have a change of scene (as my creativity had been blocked as well, and I was bored beyond belief), so I booked a flight from my home in New Mexico to North Carolina to visit my daughter and grandchildren. I felt as if I was going against a loving tide that was indeed assisting me, but I did it nonetheless. Much to my amusement, during my flight, I found myself seated in between two prison guards in transit for work related activities, and they did not even know each other! My protective custody status had remained intact— even outside of my box. (It is when we get completely "ousted," that the strange feeling of vulnerability can set in. But if we remember that things are being navigated from a loving source beyond our conscious selves, this alone can ease these uncomfortable feelings a bit—indeed, a true test of trust!)

While in this stage of "the in-between," another common development frequently occurs. If we are highly creative individuals, we may find that we need to be doing something with our energy (and not all of us want to travel to North Carolina). Even though our creativity may be blocked, it is not easy for a creative person to remain idle. If we are not used to staying put and being idle, we may endure so much, and then eventually burst out and move forward nonetheless. We simply have to make something, or *anything* happen — especially if our "in-between" stage lasts for an unusually lengthy period. So then, one day we may decide that we are going to start a new career as a botanist, or we may suddenly decide to take up photography. The next week we might say, "I've finally got it! I'm going to be a pilot!" Or perhaps we begin to wonder if we were meant to be an author or dance instructor, but for some unknown reason, we had just not realized it until now. Our loved ones (if we have any left), may be supportive or simply nod as they hear yet another brainstorm about what we are going to do next with our lives. But if they are loving souls, they may also realize that we have indeed lost our bearings, and rightfully so. When "the in-between" stage is finally complete, it will become very clear what we are here to do and be in our next phase, and we can easily find ourselves laughing at all the new careers and self-expressions we had envisioned for ourselves in times past. These attempts at holding onto a shore while we travel through the birth canal are very common, but we are not able to, nor was it planned, that we stay at any of these shores along the way. We will eventually come to find that our final shore is perfect and amazing, and very unlike anything we have experienced before. It is then as well, that grace and gratitude find us, as we come to know that the wait and frustration was all worth it.

A massive amount of change is occurring. Much— and I mean much, is being remolded and reformed on the planet, and this includes us as well. We may contract an illness or repeated bouts of the flu that insist we stay down and out of the way for a long period. We may break a bone or throw our backs out, again, making us stay put during this massive process of remolding. Another common circumstance involves our finances. We may find it nearly impossible to receive monies owed to us, to receive any kind of assistance when needed, or to have anyone remotely hear us or pay attention to our needs. When experiencing the "in-between," we are indeed in suspended animation and in this way, invisible on the earth plane. We are being prohibited from moving forward, as our new space is not yet ready and neither are we. Having things manifest for us then, or even receiving anything at this time, can be a very rare event. In this way, everything seems to go in the direction of the other party—leaving us feeling completely forgotten and non-existent.

So not only are we held back because we need to reformulate and remold the energies within ourselves, but the energies and/or the platform or grid where we will eventually land is sometimes not ready for us either. Earthquakes, floods, fires, and the like, or rather Earth changes, also occur frequently during the End Times, and these events are here for a very good reason. Although flooding, tornadoes, hurricanes, and fires offer cleansing for the planet, earthquakes have a different purpose entirely. The earthquakes during the End Times occur at very deep levels, and many times are deep enough to shift the axis on which the earth rotates (all part of the divine plan). So not only are the inhabitants of the earth required to adjust their own personal energy at deep levels in order to match the earth, but the earth herself is also re-aligning and being reborn as well. In addition, when the earth experiences these intense quakes, she is also opening herself or aligning herself to accept more light arriving from the heavens. So in these ways, there are also times when we are prohibited from moving forward until the earth herself has created a new space for our arrival. Like a perfect sailboat tacking on the ocean, we change and the earth changes— all destined to create new and higher vibrating ways of existence in a very new world, as the old world completes its death process.

These phases of being held back almost always have a natural by-product of changing long standing behavior patterns within us (especially those health related situations that keep us down). During the latter stages of the First Phase of the ascension process, there finally came a time when those who had served the planet for their entire lives, were set free and done with their service here on Earth. This meant that it was now time for them to stop helping others, to stop giving of themselves, and to now focus on creating their own world and reality, all specific to each and every one of them.

In order to change these deep-seated behavior patterns of service within these souls, much internal adjusting was needed. For some, they contracted illnesses and ailments forcing them to stay down, which prohibited them from serving and assisting others, as was their natural way of being in times past. Simply giving love and caring to others was another natural way of being, but because this love had been abused, disrespected, and drained from them along the way, this way of being needed to be altered as well. These patterns within these evolved souls then needed to be turned inward instead of outward—they needed to direct it toward themselves. Because of all the massive change needed, these souls were assisted in making these internal changes by strange occurrences manifesting as illness, ailments, and at other times, rejecting behavior from loved ones. At their higher soul levels, they were lovingly and purposely guided into moving on to their next levels, or rather new spaces—and these new spaces were now all about them, instead of everyone else.

Our spiritual evolutionary process indeed mimics menopause. With hot flashes, sleep disturbances, short-term memory loss, abdominal weight gain, depression, anxiety, and more, we are now at the phase where we are done with "the family" so to speak and need to take time for ourselves. And we especially need to *give* to ourselves. In these ways, if we are women, we may find that taking a variety of remedies for physical menopause symptoms has absolutely no desired effect, as these symptoms are a result of the ascension process, and not a result of the physical experience of menopause. So then, during the time of "the in-between," we may find that we are being remolded to now tend to ourselves and create what we have always dreamed about; and we may also find that these dreams were buried so deep within us that we were not even conscious of what they were.

4

THAWING OUT... NOW WHERE DO I GO?

SHE BEGAN TO GET DIZZY and weak. She couldn't think. Her blood sugar was dropping— she knew the symptoms well. Unusually sensitive, if she did not eat soon, her energy would suddenly crash, forcing her to eat the first thing that came across her radar. Watching for signs along the road for anything that would offer some kind of sustenance, a sign finally caught her eye. 'Mitzy's Café. Voted #1 by truckers. 3 miles ahead.'

Off to her right, Laura noticed a small farmhouse in the distance. A simple and discreet lake stood by, nearly touching the barn alongside it, and with a scattering of majestic trees nestled into the mix, a pseudo oasis emerged. She imagined a young woman at the stove preparing a home-cooked meal for her husband. As he entered the front door, taking a break from livestock and chores, he removed a sweat-stained hat with his thickly calloused hand and placed it on the wall hook by the side of the door. A broad smile soon spread across his face. He was in his favorite place now—the place he held deep within his heart—he was home. Hearing the front screen slam, the woman turned to see her husband. With a worn cotton apron tied snuggly around her waist and holding a wooden spoon now perched in mid-air, an illuminating smile spread across her face, filled with love and gratitude. She was full now, and everything was as it should be. "Am I only dreaming?" Laura wondered aloud as the lyrics to an old song made their way into her thoughts—thoughts now occupied with a reality existing far outside of her own. As she became enmeshed within her vision, her eyes began to fill with tears.

She had found herself spending more time than ever daydreaming of late. Her world had become so unpleasant, confusing, and unpredictable, that imagining things had become the only way she could find comfort—comfort within the world of her mind. The world she had left behind had become strangely and suddenly uninhabitable.

'Mitzy's Café.' There it was; a small forest green, wooden building on her right with a shiny metal roof. Three long windows overlooked the small gravel parking area in front. 'Chicken fried steak, homemade pies, and the best liver and onions in Cadron County!' *was proudly painted on the middle window. "Must be for travelers," Laura thought, as locals would already know this if it were indeed true. With so many unpredictable and traumatic events occurring for her in recent times, her trust level had plummeted within the past few months. She frequently found herself unable to move forward with the confidence and certainty she had possessed in the past. "You will always know a good café," her grandfather once told her, "by how many pick-up trucks are parked outside." Hmmmm. Well, there were two, but maybe it was only because it was long after a normal breakfast hour.*

71

The need to eat had taken a strong precedence. She would have to stop here no matter what she found inside. With her usual will and brave exterior still intact, Laura pulled the car onto the gravel parking area, shut off the engine, and opened the door. She did not realize how long she had been in the same sitting position until she straightened her legs and began walking. Stiff, weak, and wobbly, her legs felt unfamiliar beneath her, letting her know they had not been in use for quite some time. Walking was the only indication that she had been stiff and frozen for far too long.

Jingle! Jingle! Two bells on the front door dutifully and gently announced her arrival as she pulled back the heavy door and stepped inside. The familiar smell of cooking, with thick grease and a mixture of coffee, fried meat, and a subtle whiff of freshly baked pastry filled her nostrils. Reminiscent of what she had just left behind, she subconsciously braced herself for her old reality—the old reality of deep sadness, rude behavior, and stressful, confusing rejection. Preparing for an all-familiar unkindness to appear, seeing an empty booth just ahead, she robotically stepped in its direction.

"I'll be right with you!" came a shout from behind the kitchen counter. Eying an empty booth directly under one of the front windows, Laura eased her way across the dining room and slid across the vinyl seat, settling in with a view of the landscape beyond. She wasn't there but a few moments when a middle-aged woman appeared, placing a clear plastic glass of ice water, a straw, and a well-worn plastic covered menu on the table. Short in stature and wearing a pair of comfortable jeans with a tailored shirt buttoned to the top, she looked very much at home, relaxed and in charge.

"Hi, I'm Lucy. I'm short-handed today!" she lamented. "Mary's at home with her youngest—sick with that flu you know. Everybody seems to be gettin' it. Today it's just me, holdin' down the fort. I'm cookin' AND serving. Thank the Lord it's been slow all day. Just let me know when

you're ready to order. Lunch special is meatloaf, potatoes, and green beans for $4.95. Be back in a jiff!"

Laura could not remember when anyone had said that many words to her all at once, let alone in such an open, communicative, and caring way. She had felt invisible and unacknowledged for so long that she had eventually become accustomed to it. Slowly and without even knowing it, she had retreated into her own world. There was an interaction present here that she had not experienced since things had gone awry. There was room for a dialogue—a real dialogue; so unlike the many monologue conversations she had become accustomed to in recent times.

Still not ready for food, she poured over the menu looking for some kind of appetizer. By the time Lucy reappeared, she had settled on the soup of the day: Chicken noodle with saltines and water to drink. "Is that all you're havin'? A grown woman such as yourself? Are you sure you don't want a Swiss cheeseburger and fries, or maybe some of my special chili? Somethin' to stick to your ribs?" Lucy was not accustomed to light eaters in her neck of the woods, and certainly not quiet ones.

"Uh, no that's all," Laura answered demurely. "Just let me know if you change your mind. I can whip up anything else for you in no time." As Lucy walked away, Laura stared out the window, and with nothing else to think about, her thoughts turned to her grandmother. Her closest and dearest friend, they had spent many long hours together. Grocery shopping had become a very regular part of their time together. Laura loved helping her grandmother with the shopping, as it had become increasingly difficult for her grandmother to shop by herself. Her heart condition was worsening and long trips down the grocery aisle had begun to tire her to the point of exhaustion.

"I've never seen anyone talk to so many strangers in all my life!" her grandmother often chided her with a twinkle in her light blue eyes. "You strike up a conversation with everyone and anyone, and by the time we leave the store, you know everyone here! Why, it's a miracle we ever get done with the shopping at all!" But secretly Laura knew that her grandmother cherished these times. A quiet and demure woman, she welcomed the chance to meet so many new and different personalities, and these shopping trips were the highlight of her week. Oh, those were the days. When Laura was open, friendly, jovial, and loved people. And they had always, but always, loved her back.

With no book to keep her company while she ate (she had jumped in the car so impulsively, taking so little with her!), Laura looked around the café, curiosity filling her mind as it often did. Yes, it was a quiet time for the café. The only other occupied booth was one at the far end near the kitchen door. Two men sat on opposing sides of the table, sipping coffee and engaged in what appeared to be a familiar conversation. Both wore well-worn blue jeans, ropers scuffed to a comfortable perfection, button down shirts with crisp collars, and one had his shirt sleeves rolled up with a relaxed ease that seemed to say, "I'm open for business and willing to talk." As she continued to scan the room, two cowboy hats caught her eye as they hung in their reserved places on the hat tree by the front door. Everything was in order and in its usual place in this calm, steady, and relaxed café amidst lush green meadows, wide expansive sky, and cattle who held steady all day, heads down, doing what they knew best—grazing.

Jingle! Jingle! The door suddenly flew open, and a young woman burst in, her long blond hair flying behind her. "Hey Lucy! Damian is down with that darn flu and I have to go to Littleton today. Do you have any soup handy so's I can get him fed before I go? I made some blueberry corn muffins for ya, in case you were runnin' low. Was all out of soup ingredients though." From the far booth, the man with the rolled up shirt sleeves immediately turned his head her way. "Jody, tell Damian I can come by later this afternoon and tend to the feeding if he needs it. I'll give him a holler later on." As the corn muffins and soup changed hands, and Jody *flew back out the door, the subtle ripple of a problem had been smoothed out, almost as if it had never happened at all.*

Feeling an outsider in a strange land, Laura finished her soup quickly, eager to get back on the road and into her own familiar space in the car. "You come back and see us again!" called Lucy as Laura opened the heavy door. Feeling the brightness of the sun upon her face, she felt a very subtle shift. Ever so slowly, her numbness was thawing, unable to withstand the warmth of love and caring, even if she tried.

. . .

After so much loss and emptiness, we can become frozen and stuck, stiff from an inability to move forward and now seemingly accustomed to a new pattern of continued departures with no arrivals. It can become near impossible to even remember when something new sprang forth, or when we last created a new project, as our souls have somehow strangely become barren while we sit in a confusing emptiness, wondering what in the world is occurring. And the love—where has it gone? I remember a period when I was deep in the midst of this stage of losing my life. Each time I thought that this would be the end of all the losses, the next thing would depart. The list began to feel endless. With my usual creativity compromised, my life, house, and adobe walled-in acre seemed stark and hollow— like a dungeon at the depths of the unknown. It was my first spring season in my new home—a home that was not yet landscaped, and I dearly missed having more of nature around me. My physical environment had now begun to match my emotional one.

One day I looked out my kitchen window and noticed a bird building a nest on top of a sconce in the alcove near the front door. With much of everything else feeling so lifeless in recent times, the nest and mother bird stood out in stark contrast, like something from another world that I had not experienced for a very long time. New life—a small bird in a small corner of my space, bringing back my usual passion for *life*—if only with a small and simple spark.

Soon, the nest began to take a solid shape and the bird began to sit in it. Eggs! There was new life soon to arrive in my space, and for me, it felt like a holy moment. Each time I looked out my window and gazed at the bird, my eyes filled with grateful tears at the arrival of such a beautiful display of nature—a sweet mother bird sitting with her young the way God had intended. There were no trees in my yard (not uncommon in New Mexico, with sagebrush plentiful), but this bird had arrived nonetheless and found a sheltered space near the front door. I felt so blessed! When repair people arrived, I made them use the back door…my honorable guests were not to be disturbed. And when ravaging windstorms howled and sand blew, I would run to the window, praying that the bird and her eggs had remained intact, still safe and secure.

Craving this beautiful energy and so grateful that it had arrived, I soon became very attached to the nest and mother bird. Several times a day, I would look out my window and feel a very welcome companionship. Gradually the bird began to fly up to the window where I stood, and in time, she would come to perch on the other sconce by the front door, which was much closer to the kitchen window. If there had not been a screen between us, I could have reached out and touched her golden belly as we exchanged greetings throughout the day. In time, we began to engage in a strange conversation of sounds, her magnificent face now clearly visible in great detail. With her strong and pointed beak poised ever so prominently with a dignified confidence, her intent gaze in my direction created a much-needed connection— and a new sense of normal, as nothing else had felt remotely right in recent times.

One day I looked out and saw two tiny heads bobbing, mouths wide open when mama arrived. At other times, all was quiet while the babies remained tucked securely in their small nest, sleeping away the day. The eggs had finally hatched. After some research, I was able to identify the bird as a Western King. At times, mama bird would sit on the opposing roof, screeching at any impending danger, as she watched over her young. One day, a family of quail paraded through the front gate and onward into the yard with many tiny offspring dutifully following behind their mother, resulting in a severe scolding by mama Western King. At other times during the day, mama bird would soar around the property in wide, expansive circles, making the most beautiful sounds I had heard in far too long. During a thunderstorm late one night, it became suddenly quiet as the rain ceased. But in the aftermath, I heard mama King bird soaring as she often did. The intense crackling of thunder, the brilliant lightning in sudden piercing displays, and the pounding of the rain had finally ceased, and she was free to emerge once again. Soaring, soaring through the sky under a full moon, making her now familiar territorial sounds, she was simply doing what she did best. The wide-open sky was her home, and she accepted this with no reservations. She was free here, and this particular space above my own, was now her space as well. Tearing up as I lay under the covers, I was ever so grateful for the companionship of this very new family that I had grown to love.

My favorite memory of mama King bird was what ultimately led to the beginning of my thawing out stage. With the onset of spring, the sun had begun to set farther in the west. During a few moments each day, the sun was positioned so that it would shine blaringly and very directly at the bird nest. And it had begun to get hot during that time as well. Each day during these few moments of blaring sun, mama bird would glide in from seemingly nowhere, landing gracefully on the nest. The babies were beginning to grow by this time, and had become almost too big to fit in the small nest. Their shaggy heads would pop up from time to time, and they were beginning to resemble their mother in size. But each day, she would arrive during that exact moment of blazing sun, perch herself on the edge of the nest, and spread her wings wide as she sheltered her young from the blaring sun and heat. Day after day, she would arrive during the same time of blaring sun, wings spread as full and wide as she could stretch them, until the sun had dropped below the horizon, and then she would depart. Dedicated to her mission of protecting her young from the intense heat, she did it seemingly without question, as it was her innate instinct to do so. Her innocent babies, unable to protect themselves, and too young to know how, were receiving love and caring in a most majestic, beautiful, and natural way.

This was the first time that I had experienced love and caring in my space during my time of great losses. Having so much loss occur in such a short time was indeed challenging, but the lack of love was by far the most challenging of all. This instinct of love and caring had all but been lost in human beings of late, and my heart was deeply touched as I watched the birds each day. To see the natural instinct of love and caring still intact, if even within the bird community, gave me a renewed hope and new connection... heart energy in a dark night that had gone on for far too long.

Eventually, the Western King family successfully moved on, but by this time, I had acquired bird feeders and a birdbath in my back yard, and after a long period of waiting, a wide range of birds eventually arrived. Even though there were now several varieties of birds coming daily to the back yard, my experience with the Western King birds was so much more personal, intimate, and meaningful, that there was no comparison. The Western Kings had brought me the heart energy, and in this way, I was now able to connect to the energy of the new world. The universe had indeed validated that God's love was ever-present, and this love had arrived in the form of these very special birds.

Once the thawing out period begins, and we start to experience warmth, caring, support, and love once again, it can feel as if we are getting a much-needed drink after an eternity in the desert. The stage of thawing out does not arrive until we have lost enough of what we need to lose in order to enable us to move forward and out of our old spaces. Whether through being kicked out, from being turned away through unpleasant and disrespectful behavior, or abandoned through death, no matter how it occurs, we must move into the new space of the new world if we are to remain on the planet in times to come.

As was intended, experiencing great loss has a graceful and holy by-product as well. Not only then, do we experience loss as a means of placing us in very new and better spaces, but this heartbreaking loss has another distinct purpose as well. As our hearts break over and over again—whether due to a deep sadness about conditions on the planet, from the losses of loved ones who are not yet ready to move forward and experience love themselves, or even perhaps from the loss of our loving human and animal companions who have decided to depart early— *a broken heart also creates an open heart.* And there is yet another by-product that arrives, which vibrates nearly as high as love, and that is gratitude. With so many losses having occurred for many of us, we eventually become oh so grateful for the smallest and simplest displays of caring and kindness. Bringing us to states of simplicity, where we come to know what is really and truly important in life, gratitude is a key component in this process. This divine plan of spiritual evolution may not appear to be unfolding properly, but I can assure you, as always, it is. This is the way the inhabitants of the earth have ultimately chosen to create a more evolved human being, and also, how they have chosen to create the climate necessary for a new world to unfold. We are moving forward and evolving, and even though the ascension road has repeatedly been adjusted, tweaked, and molded in accordance with the current planetary climate, we will most certainly arrive at our intended destination no matter how the inhabitants of the earth have chosen to get there. Having our hearts open then, through the experience of heartbreak, is one of the tweaks and adjustments that was made along the way. Experiencing heartbreak, along with a wearing down through loss of power and unpleasant circumstances, if even a more unpleasant, harsh, and challenging way than was originally intended, is where we are now.

As we evolve then, we will be removed from situations and energies where there is no love, the more that we embody love ourselves. Our environment must match what we are now embodying ourselves, so if it does not, we will separate. This process will eventually create new spaces where loving hearts will begin to congregate, while others are denied access until they are being and embodying this love themselves. In addition, with hearts now wide open, many are poised to receive more light within as never before. Just as the earth herself is opening via deep-seated earthquakes— through broken hearts, we will ourselves open as well. Together then, the earth and the inhabitants who have been willing to experience heart-opening changes, will be repositioned into a very new world and new reality— the earth through a repositioning on her axis from the deep earthquakes, and her inhabitants through deep heart openings now re-positioning them into very new spaces.

After our hearts begin to open, we almost immediately begin to experience related symptoms that validate that this is indeed occurring. Below is a list of some of the most common symptoms (as always, it is best to consult a qualified health practitioner if one is experiencing an ailment, as these ailments are not always attributed to the ascension process):

- *Weeping.* As our hearts begin to open, we can find ourselves crying at the drop of a hat and for just about any reason. A gifted numerologist once told me, that in 2009, I may have complained about crying 24/7, but according to my chart, I would not be crying at all in 2010. I think I cried even more in 2010! This is because ascension and its symptoms defies and overrides all else. And again, mimics menopause in this regard: we become emotional. We are going through change and we cry easily during this time as our hearts are opening.

- *Lung pain.* We may find it difficult to breathe and/or experience pain when breathing. As our hearts break open and expand, energy moves out. This causes inflammation and discomfort in the areas surrounding the heart. Painful breathing may come and go as our hearts open at intervals. We may become weak in our lung areas as well, making us more susceptible to bronchitis, pneumonia, allergies, or other lung related disorders. Again, it is always best to consult a health care professional if experiencing any lung disorders.

- *Heart pain.* We may feel that something very heavy is sitting on our chest, that we cannot breathe, and at times, we may experience heart palpitations. And not to forget the very general and persistent *heart ache.* Our hearts are on over-drive as they begin to open and receive the new energy. And again, please, please consult a qualified health care professional if you are experiencing any scary heart related symptoms, as they cannot always be attributed to the ascension process— but the majority of the time they are indeed ascension related.

- *Esophagus burning and tightness.* As this area is so close to the heart, it can experience inflammation when the heart begins to open and expand. Staying away from acidic foods and taking any kind of acid reducing herbs can greatly assist with this pain and tightness. It can feel as if it is difficult to swallow as well, as digesting and swallowing the current earth conditions have become most unpleasant for some of us. There is a condition diagnosed by allopathic doctors called *Global Hysteria.* Feeling as if there is a lump in one's throat, similar to the feeling of wanting to cry but holding it back, are symptoms of this disorder. A good cry can alleviate *Global Hysteria*, and an ant-acid greatly helps with esophagus burning and pressure.

- *Pain between the shoulder blades.* A very common symptom of heart opening, or what I used to refer to as growing our angel wings. As they begin to sprout, or rather as our hearts begin to open, it is quite common to experience this upper back pain.

- *Neck stiffness.* A common experience for many years in regard to the ascension process, having a very stiff neck is still a forerunning symptom. Higher energy moving through the spine area where our angel wings sprout causes this malady.

- *A subtle feeling of hysteria.* This is an emotional feeling, and not a physical one. Great change and expansion are occurring on the planet, and as the energy that creates this movement arrives, it can create feelings of hysteria when it hits us. We may also feel overwhelmed for no particular reason…and just plain hysterical. Great movement, great change, and great losses can be overwhelming. For those highly sensitive, this hysteria energy may not always be their own, but is simply being picked up from the outside.

- *Feeling deeply wounded by the lower vibrating energies.* This is not our ego talking…it is our heart. At times when experiencing disrespect and uncaring, I would immediately cry. I was not crying for me, but for the state of the planet and how wounded I felt within my heart. These lower vibrating energies can wound our hearts beyond measure, and we may find ourselves clutching our hands to our chests and weeping tears of sadness after we have an encounter with a heartless energy.

After so much heartbreak, we eventually begin the process of thawing out. Very suddenly, we may find that we are able to feel again after being frozen and stuck for a very long time. The process of great losses and removal from so much can take as long as it needs to take. But when it is finally complete, or at least fairly near completion, we will begin to feel quite different. As we begin to enter the new phase of finally moving forward, subtle shifts begin to occur.

We may find ourselves singing for no apparent reason, where in times past singing was about the last thing we could ever imagine ourselves doing. We may finally be ready for a very new haircut or new look. We may suddenly want to re-decorate our home. Strange as it sounds, light bulbs may burnout in unusual epidemic proportions, as batteries go dead as well—both needing replacement as we fill our new spaces with a new energy. And fixing, fixing, fixing…we may find ourselves fixing everything in sight as we continue with this preparedness. We may find ourselves laughing easily and at least laughing again, as in times past grieving seemed to be our only emotion. We may feel lighter and more free, almost as if we have lifted up from the bottom of a hole. We won't be so touchy, and our creativity usually returns as well—enabling us to finally be ready to bring forth something new. But most importantly, we will suddenly find ourselves breathing deeply, filling our lungs to capacity with deep breaths, as we are grateful once again to be on the earth at this time.

We have now created a new us and are now ready then, for a very new space on the planet. But what if there is nowhere on the planet that remotely resembles who and what we are now about? Where in the world do we go now?

5

THE CHILDREN... OUR BRIDGE TO HEAVEN

THE CHILDREN. OUR MOST precious commodity—our most valuable resource—our greatest gift. The children are our gift from heaven, and in this way, they are indeed the bridge to the other side, as they are heaven itself.

They have purposely come to the earth during this special time, and at their soul levels, they know very well what they have come to accomplish. They carry this wisdom deep within themselves and are dedicated to their purpose. Many of our children are very advanced souls who would not be here if it were not time for their unusual presence. *Very real* and very naturally connected to higher ways of living and being than most of the adult residents of the planet, the children are here to raise us up and connect us to a higher level of existence through our own unique connection to *them*.

Each generation of our children carries its own unique blueprint and purpose, but as time progresses, the next generation continues to produce a more advanced soul than the one prior. And being that the earth is in an intense state of evolution, these young people carry the distinct purpose and energy that the earth needs at the time of their birth. Our next to the newest generation is very direct, sensitive, at times aggressive, and they know exactly what they want. They can spot love a mile away, and will very naturally gravitate toward it. They operate through feeling energy, so at times they will shy away from some energies and move toward others. And they are very active as well, as they are filled with an energy that needs a continual outlet. Our newest children, being born around 2011, carry the energy of the heart. They are sweet, loving, calm, and when you look at them, they simply look like one big valentine! They are all about love, emit this energy in all ways as it radiates from them like a loving current here to shift us all, and are purely and simply one big love-bug.

Our children are without question more evolved than we adults are. Because they arrive very ready and in tandem with the current energies of the planet, our newest generation is all about love. Highly revered by all energies on the planet, the more highly vibrating unseen energies are in a magical awe of our little ones. To them, our children are royalty, and for very good reason.

After my twin grandsons were born, I had the pleasure and excitement of coming to North Carolina to meet them. Having two new premature babies just home from the NICU, my daughter, her husband, and I had our hands full seemingly around the clock. One afternoon, I took a fussy Solomon outside for a change of venue, as I could not seem to calm him. With nature now surrounding us, I will never forget the instant change and shift that soon occurred. Now outside in nature, the nature kingdom immediately took notice—and so did Solomon. The nature kingdom and all its fairies and divine creatures of the earth, will most usually stay back and hide. They will indeed reveal themselves if they sense that it is safe to do so, and many times it will take them a while to come out nonetheless. With Solomon in my arms, it was a very different story.

It was as if a trumpet had sounded, and all the nature spirits came to immediate attention. With a most humble demeanor, they presented themselves in great awe, and made it clear how fortunate they were to have Solomon in their presence. For them, he was a gift from God— he was royalty in their eyes—a rare and revered presence in their world. They knew where he originated—from the far-away heavens—and they also knew that he possessed an energy rarely seen on the planet until now. He had come from very far away, as it was now time. A place so very far away, that it was a heaven into itself and had not connected to this earth at any time before. Solomon immediately calmed down as well, as he now seemed to feel completely at home.

Two and a half years later, when I returned to North Carolina to make it my home, I took my family for a walk in the forest along the river. With massive icicles hanging from gorgeous rocky cliffs, snow on the ground, and an immeasurable beauty all around us, the children were nearly giddy to be among nature so eloquently presenting itself. But the babies were ecstatic—as if they were home at last. "Wahdo! Wahdo!" they exclaimed at the sight of the river, and when it was time to turn back on the trail towards home, they became hysterical with many tears and great resistance. "No! No! No!" they cried. As if they were being yanked away from a precious comfort zone of familiarity, peace, and love, they did not want to part from what they knew deep inside themselves as home.

But the most memorable moment for me, was what occurred when we began our entrance into the forest. I had completely forgotten about the reaction of the nature spirits a few years prior when Solomon was a small infant. I had been on this trail many times before when I first arrived in North Carolina. Each time, I was stopped at the entrance by a non-physical "gatekeeper" and given an escort. But when I arrived with the babies, a totally different scenario unfolded. As we entered the forest, they immediately presented themselves in awe and reverence, and many of the older and wiser spirits wrapped their energy around the children in waves of protection. (Hey—why hadn't I ever been welcomed this way? Sniff, sniff.) Our precious cargo and most valuable resource— the children— had arrived, and even the nature spirits acknowledged this event in their own special way.

The children are the bridge to the new world and to the new energy, as they very naturally embody it themselves. They are our shining stars, our glimpse into heaven, and the road to get there. Our youngest little ones come from a place in the cosmos where the earth and her inhabitants have not been before. They know this new position then, far better than we do—this new position, or new "home" for us all, is precisely where they originated. So in this way, they can easily connect us. Like a cord to the infinite, we need only grab on and allow them to take us to a very new shore. We are so blessed to have them here in our presence; their arrival here is an unprecedented event.

Many adults in recent times have found themselves estranged from their adult children, which means that they are estranged from their grandchildren as well. Many times for reasons unknown, their adult children have refused to speak to them or to continue any kind of connection. As we have learned through the process of arriving in a new world, our loved ones may disconnect from us so that we will be free to move on into a new space where we rightfully belong. This is very common. And at times, we may be the ones who initiate the disconnect, as we are no longer able or willing to tolerate the lower vibrating behaviors and energy that they embody.

One way to find our way back to our adult children is through their own children, or our grandchildren. At times, some may find themselves prohibited from connecting to their grandchildren, but know that these special children are serving as a bridge nonetheless. They are holding the space until the right time when a connection will again be possible. At their soul levels, these children know exactly what is up. They remain with their parents in order to assist them with their own evolution simply by their presence, and are willing at their highest levels to provide this assistance.

When my daughter and I found our way back to each other, and with a new and very different relationship, it was the children that served as the bridge. With a mutual love and great reverence for these little ones, we were able to meet in the middle—and love was, of course, the glue. I was fortunate that she knew how much I loved my grandchildren, as she loved them too, and allowed me to visit them very often. We are now a big happy family again, but the brief disconnect my daughter and I experienced was a vitally important step in creating a very new and different family dynamic—all based on love. When we reunited again as a whole, it was a whole that was now in alignment with the new world and its energies of love, respect, and deep caring.

The children then, are the bridge to the new world and heaven here on earth, as well as the bridge to the energies that are lagging behind. They are very special indeed. In this way, we may find ourselves inexplicably drawn to children and even craving them. The only time we may feel remotely normal during this massive transition, is when we are in their presence. They carry the blueprint and energy of heaven on Earth, so this would only be natural. I will never forget a time when I was in "the in-between" and connected to…well…not a thing I suppose. I had gone to my daughter's house to play with my grandchildren. With a large grassy area behind her home dropping off to a creek, it was a great place to play. While we danced and sang, and skipped and ran, I suddenly found myself looking up toward the house where the babies were headed. Four tiny legs bobbing to and fro, they ran up the hill in front of me, with a slow and elegant grace. With lush grass surrounding us, and fragile new flowers interspersed here and there, seeing these pure and innocent beings frolicking ahead of me while I came from behind, brought tears to my eyes. With their miniature bodies, bare feet, caramel skin, and glowing faces, I felt I had indeed landed in heaven on Earth.

If we are ready for a connection to the children, it will indeed find its way to us. When I first arrived in North Carolina, I began looking for a rental home. Without exception, each home I found was either across the street from an elementary school, a playground, or some kind of facility where children were ever-present. Very quickly, I was blessed to find the perfect home of my dreams, and it was, of course, looking out over a beautiful place in nature where children frequented daily. Some solicitors came to the door recently, and after I declined their offering, they turned to go. One of the women suddenly stopped, turned around, and asked, "This is such a beautiful, beautiful spot. Does the sound of the children get loud?" "Oh, no!" I could only reply. "It is a beautiful sound—the sound of children." And my neighbors have expressed the same.

Until enough of the planet is embodying the new energy of the heart and higher ways of living and being, the children will serve as the bridge to the other side. In this way, if we do not know where to go after we have lost so much, we can always go where the children are. They deserve to be our top priority, to have our reverence and dedication, and can teach us much. We can follow the energy of the children when feeling lost and hanging in the balance, as they are wonderful guideposts for the energies of the other side. But what if we are still feeling lost and unsure about most things in our life? With so much crashing and leaving, how do we know what to do next or where to go? Following signs from above that are lovingly presented to us each and every day can greatly help.

6

FOLLOWING THE SIGNS

LAURA HAD BEEN DRIVING for several days, developing a comfortable pattern of driving, stopping to eat, and finding a simple but decent place to spend the night as the sun dropped below the horizon. She was grateful for this predictable structure, if even modest. It was just what she needed. And being behind the wheel all day gave her a new feeling of control—something she had not felt for a very long time. She had subconsciously begun to exhale throughout the day, blowing out large billows of air through puckered lips, as though she was nearing a final phase of emptying out—clearing out the last remnants of the old. And it felt good. Her hands had begun to relax on the steering wheel, freeing her to reach out ever so slightly to adjust the tuner on the radio, now occasionally listening to local music as she watched each small town disappear through her rear view mirror.

It had begun to get warm this day, and Laura's feet began to itch and prickle as each toe filled and expanded with new circulation, slowly moving its way upward through her stiff body. Her face soon flushed. Taking off her sweater and placing it in the back of the car, she realized Bernie's empty space had become a more familiar sight, soon to be filled by a sweater no longer needed. Rolling down the windows and opening her sunroof, new smells of spring filled her nostrils. She inhaled deeply, each deep breath filling her body from her now warm toes to the tips of her fingers. Flowers. The air now smelled of flowers.

Almost as quickly as it began to warm up, the terrain began to change. Vast meadows surrounded by Ponderosa pine began looming up from the distant horizon. Accompanied by white billowy clouds filling a perfect azure sky as far and vast as the eye could see, the air was crisp and clean —the air of a very new land. Horses with sleek coats in varying colors were scattered here and there, as they grazed contentedly, heads down and nostrils flared. A soft breeze filled the air, and as new and stronger gusts arrived, the horses raised their heads, manes flowing in the breeze, tails stretched out behind them, as they galloped with abandon, running free across the meadowlands.

She had reached southwest Colorado.

"If only I can push on," Laura thought to herself, "I might find a perfect town just like my old town, only with better circumstances, and then I could relocate." On she drove, passing new meadowlands not sporadically filled with horses now, but with wide expanses of wild flowers. White, yellow, pink, and purple, color filled the land like an artist's pallet waiting for just the right brush to lay a new foundation. Cresting a hill, the terrain suddenly shifted again, for on the other side of the hill lay a small, quaint village, nestled at the foot of majestic snow capped peaks, alongside a rushing river weaving its way through pines, small storefronts, and carefully placed footbridges.

"What a beautiful place," Laura thought, "But this is a very small village. I need stores, conveniences, connections, and cities nearby if I am to earn a living! And how do I know that the people here are good and caring — not self-absorbed and arrogant? Too big of a risk. And this place feels too different from what I am accustomed to anyway. What would I DO here?!"

She continued to drive. Her instincts had seemingly betrayed her in the past and she no longer trusted them. Determined to find a better place and something that she could relate to, she suddenly noticed she had driven straight through a red light—the only stoplight at the far edge of town. "Oops! I can't believe I didn't see that stoplight! Too intent on finding a new spot I guess," she mumbled as she drove out of town, her self-confidence dropping even further. As she looked in her rear view mirror, as she had done so many times before when leaving small towns behind, there was something new this time—the flashing lights of a police car approaching her. The red traffic light she had run! Her heart sank. Now she was going to get a ticket —her first ticket ever. "Things are never going to change. I am still being attacked by ugliness!" Laura screeched to herself as she pulled over to the side of the road.

The officer had only issued her a verbal warning ("Don't you know that a stop light means STOP?"), but it was enough to warrant a quick breather. Laura was ready for a brief time-out. Even a stop by the police was too much excitement for her these days. The predictable new pattern she had established for each day had already been disrupted. "I'm just going to sit here and rest for a minute," she thought to herself. "I don't know what is going on. I don't trust my usual instincts anymore. Every time I attempt to add something to my life, it's taken away. And now I am pulled over by the police! Where is my usual normal and where is some predictability…ANY predictability?"

95

Putting her seat in the reclining position, she leaned back, exhaled deeply, and closed her eyes. There was that smell again…the sweet and subtle smell of flowers. She slowly opened her eyes and looked off to her right. And there it was. A meadow filled with wildflowers. Rows and rows of color standing in bright contrast to lush green grass, with a radiant blanket of blue sky overhead. The beauty she had been yearning for was right in front of her—sitting simply and purely and innocently while waiting to be noticed. Her eyes were now full of new life— and a very new space. She saw it, she smelled it, and she connected to it. It was here all along, only she had not been ready to see it. As she allowed herself to drift into this very new place in the cosmos, she suddenly had a strong awareness. Wait a minute…WAIT A MINUTE! Sitting bolt upright, she jerked to attention. Was the stop light trying to tell her something? Was the police officer an angel in disguise reminding her "to stop" as this village was finally right where she needed to be? Was he simply trying to help her? Was all this a sign from God?

She started the engine, turned her car around, and went back to the village.

. . .

As we begin to evolve and expand, we become much more aware. Looking through the windows of our eyes, we eventually come to see a beautiful, magical, and love-filled energy that weaves itself in and out of every single thing in existence. Although it might not seem like it at times, this love-filled energy has been there all along. When we lose much of everything through the process of dying while we remain alive, we are then placed into a very new position—and this new position allows us to be removed from a world and reality that we had come to interpret through immature eyes.

Two important mantras become ever present and crystal clear during times of great loss and immeasurable transition, and if we remember them and utilize them throughout our process, they can serve to provide something to hold onto that will always remain true:

Thank you God, for everything,
and
Everyone is always helping me.

When we are in the tunnel of transition, or "the in-between," it can be near impossible to see anything clearly. We can be the most intuitive of people, with a prior intuitive level that supersedes all other human processes, or even with a clear and succinct connection to God, but when in "the in-between," it all goes out the window. We are neither here nor there in this massive tunnel of re-birth and cannot then, see outside of its walls. It is then that we must know that we are always, and always have been, lovingly cared for and watched over from above. So although a new clearness of sight eventually returns to us when we finally land on a new and different shore, when in the tunnel of transition, if we cannot see with our normal eyes, we can always choose to see the road by looking for, acknowledging, and following the many signs that God and the universe provides.

Thank You God, For Everything

While in the midst of losing much, we may find ourselves wondering why on Earth we are being punished this way. "I don't deserve this!" may have become our new mantra. Or even, "I have come so far in my spiritual growth and am now left with nothing to show for it and nowhere to go! Something has indeed gone awry this time. Who's in charge up there anyway?!" We may feel as if we are in a small rowboat, floating out in a vast sea of nothingness, wondering where God has indeed gone. We may feel continually beaten down, unable to get our heads up for even a moment, as the energies from above continue to remove anything unlike love. We may have eventually cried out in desperation, asking for something, or anything, to arrive for us, only to be met with a rude and senseless silence.

Country western singer Garth Brooks stated it well with these lyrics in *Unanswered Prayers*:

Sometimes I thank God for unanswered prayers
Remember when you're talkin' to the man upstairs
That just because he doesn't answer doesn't mean he don't care
Some of God's greatest gifts are unanswered prayers

Some of God's greatest gifts are all too often unanswered...
Some of God's greatest gifts are unanswered prayers

As we have learned throughout this process of loss, we absolutely cannot create anything new until we have lost everything we need to lose—otherwise, we will simply re-create things that belong to our prior self who has since died. We are being re-born. And this new "us" is lovingly being prepared to arrive in a very new heaven on earth, even if it does not feel like it at times. We cannot take the old with us. We are being released then, in every way possible. In this way, we have many, many unanswered prayers during this time, as our desires cannot come from an old self (or old planet) that will soon no longer exist. After we emerge on a new and different shore, we most always find ourselves thinking, "Thank God this or that never happened! Who and what I have found now is so much better!" It seems that God knows more about our dreams than we do, or at least what is best for us at any given time.

After we have lost so much and the world no longer makes much sense to us (remember, it is being re-structured into a very new world with new and different ways of being), we can lose our self-confidence as well. We can easily become confused while this invisible force is molding, pushing, and placing us somewhere where we have never been before. And as we now know, it may also seem as though we have absolutely no control over anything at all.

In the beginning stages of our massive transition, we may feel like part of a gigantic tossed salad as we are tossed willy nilly here and there, up and down, around and around, while nothing remotely makes sense. But God is at the helm and has a hand in the entire process. And this is where faith and trust come into play. So no matter what strange and unsettling events occur for us, we can choose to believe and eventually come to a place where we *thank God for everything*.

Beatrix Potter, gifted writer of children's books, whose books have sold more than any children's books in history, was a private and sensitive soul. Never having an abundance of friends, at an older age than was normal for that time, she met and fell in love with her publisher. Shortly before they were to marry, he fell ill and died. She had finally opened her heart and now it was broken. Deeply devastated, against the wishes and concerns of her family, she purchased a large farm in the country in an area that she had always loved. Her animal companions were now not only in her books, but by her side in many ways. It was here that she moved into the next phase of her path, where she became a conservationist with a love for the land, protecting and preserving many, many acres surrounding her farm for years to come. And in time, she did indeed marry. If she had not experienced such a deep loss, she may never have moved into the next phase of her soul path as a conservationist.

Jane Austen, one of the best-selling authors of all time, had a deep conviction that she marry "for affection" and not for money or stature, as was common during that time. Although opportunities arose for her to marry for reasons of security, she nonetheless chose to marry the man of her heart, even though he could not adequately provide for them in customary ways. Through circumstances prevalent during that time, she was not able to follow through with the marriage. Her broken heart spurred her on to write novels of the heart, and these novels are still read far and wide… and loved and enjoyed by many, even after 200 years.

As mentioned throughout this book, for many of the service-oriented souls living on the planet now (or rather the souls whose path was about bringing the planet to higher ways of living and being), this path has been abruptly cut short.

Through circumstances that vary with each soul, these souls have been prohibited from continuing this planetary assistance, and greatly encouraged to now simply take care of themselves. This is the space they are being encouraged to occupy, and they deserve it. If these souls did not arrive in this space willingly, they nonetheless arrived, if even through forced circumstances—and in this way, they can choose to *thank God for everything.* These souls have now arrived in the next phase of their soul path, which involves living in heaven on Earth. Their prior purpose is complete.

God is ever-present, providing the circumstances for us to fulfill our dreams and place us in a new heaven on earth. Even though this presence is indeed here during times of great tragedy and loss, it is also here at any given moment of any given day. With all the losses, we can at times forget what we still have, and forget to be grateful for what remains. I remember days when I would check my sleeping cat to make sure she was still breathing, as it felt like she was all I had left. The sun still shines, the flowers still bloom, the rivers still run, and nature abounds. Yesterday, one of my young grandsons stopped while we were in a grassy meadow, as he spotted a worm. Picking it up, he marveled at it as he held it in his hand, eventually replacing it in its "house" under some turf. "I put it in its house Gama." Shortly thereafter, he suddenly stopped what he was doing, as he had looked up and seen a tiny sliver of moon in a daylight sky, peeking out from billowing clouds. "Look! Moon!" How he spotted it, I will never know, but soon all of us were looking up and marveling at that special sliver of moon, barely visible in a day-lit sky.

Everyone Is Always Helping Me

At our higher soul levels, we are always going in the same direction, loving and supporting each other and the entire planet. As we begin to evolve and expand, we are able to see beyond the veil on a more regular basis, and in this way, we do not become as lost and confused by the behavior of others. As our ego selves begin to diminish as well, and when so much has been cleared away from all the losses we sustain, we are then able to see more clearly what is really and truly occurring, and do not take things as personally as we might have in times past.

So in this way, even though someone may be treating us badly, we come to find that they are attempting to support us in moving on to a better place where poor treatment does not exist. I think my mantra for 2010 was, "I'm not used to being treated so badly!" I cannot count the times I spoke these words. And through all this poor treatment and tragedy, our hearts are opening through a horrific pounding. It is these seemingly unkind souls then, who are providing this pounding in order to support our evolutionary process. In this way, we can come to know that *everyone is always helping us*, even though it may feel as if just the opposite is occurring.

I remember hearing a story once, about a woman who was distraught about the passing of her mother. She had brought her mother to the emergency room, where the health care providers had served to ignore her so much, and in so many ways, that she died due to lack of attention. At higher soul levels, these health care providers were assisting the mother in passing over, which was her desire and soul plan. They were all in it together and the plan succeeded beautifully. *Everyone was helping.*

Recently, the partner of a close friend had a sudden heart attack and died. My friend had cared for him for many years, and was very distraught that he was not there at the time his partner passed over. "What would you have done if you had been there?" I asked him one day. "I would have ordered him to be resuscitated," he replied. But his partner was ready to pass over, so in this way, he chose to leave the way that he did. Even though my friend is still most upset that he was not present at the time his partner passed over, he can choose to know that he greatly helped his partner by not being there. At their soul levels, they were in on it together.

Living in New Mexico can bring with it an imminent companionship with many creatures. From tarantulas, to rattle snakes, to scorpions, to coyotes, and a wide array of raptors, the list can be quite lengthy. I had a new experience when I moved into my new home, which involved sharing it with large red centipedes. On first sight, they looked quite threatening—up to six inches long with an endless amount of legs and deadly looking pinchers. Upon investigation and from just hanging out with them, I found that they seek out moisture, feed on spiders, and seem to come out at night, while the remainder of the time they stay hidden under rugs and the like. After getting to know them, I immediately felt comfortable, as to me, they were helping rid my home of spiders, and in this way, we were now friends and on the same team. If wandering around the house in the middle of the night, I simply watched where I stepped. They had their space and I had mine. I soon dubbed them the "spider brigade." They were indeed helping me with my in-home spider population, all while I slept.

More prevalent than ever is another kind of help—the help that arrives through the words spoken by individuals who cross our path. And these words are rarely intentional, as they are usually spoken with a different meaning or message than which was intended for our particular circumstance. After I put my home in New Mexico up for sale, I received lots of nibbles but no definite offer that was appropriate. After two months, I vacated it completely and moved to North Carolina. Weeks went by as it sat empty, and I began to wonder why in the world it was taking so long to sell. With this question continually in the back of my mind, the answers soon arrived like a never-ending stream flowing along beside me. When I opened a new bank account in North Carolina, out of the blue and for no apparent reason (we were not even having a conversation), the bank teller remarked, "Just wait until spring." My son-in-law remarked out of the blue one day that his employer had just told him things would improve for the company "when spring arrives. Just hold on a little longer." In January, my real estate agent said to hold on until spring, although he does not recall saying this. My home did indeed sell the day after the spring equinox. I had received the same message so many times that it was impossible to ignore, and it gave me great comfort and reassurance as well during my time of waiting. God was speaking to me, if even through the mouths of his/her earthly angels.

When we have a dilemma present in our lives, and it remains subtly in the back of our minds waiting for resolution, the answer is given to us repeatedly through the mouths of others, or even at times, through the passage in a book or the words in a song. If we can come to a place where we know that God is always speaking to us, and know that we are all in this together, we can grow accustomed to listening for these very important and comforting messages. *Everyone is indeed, always helping us.*

Following the Signs

Another way that we continually receive guidance and messages from above, is through the many metaphors present in everyday life. These double meanings are ever-present and delivering assistance if we choose to acknowledge them. And many times, they are easy to spot by the insistence and persistent energy that surrounds them.

After I had been in "the in-between" for what felt like far too long, it was finally time to move forward once again. Hesitant, as I had been blocked repeatedly in times past, I was still lying low. Upon arriving home from a trip, my new cat-sitter invited me to her home to ride her horses. I gracefully declined. She became very insistent that I come. I gracefully declined once again, but she would not let up. Being that she was a gentle and very subtle soul, it was then that I knew something else must be occurring, so I accepted. Within a few short days, I was "back in the saddle" and not only did I love the reconnection with the horses (I love horses, but had not ridden for many years), but felt in control once again as I sat up high in communion with a large animal while at times giving direction, which greatly helped in giving me back my self-confidence. It was time to get back in the saddle. It was okay to finally move forward once again. The universe had been trying to get my attention to give me this timely message.

One day, I had a meeting with a new professional. When I arrived at the appointed time, the door to her office was open, but all the lights were off and she was not present. She was evidently "open" to the meeting, but not connected to "the light," as all the lights were off. We were never able to connect at a later date, and I soon found that her services were not needed after all and she would not have been a good fit for me.

But metaphors are not our only clues. My daughter and I have a fun game we play after we watch a movie. We read the credits at the end, and almost always find our names listed. She has an unusual name, but finds it many times nonetheless. The titles attached to our names and the names of the people we know, always seem to match who and what the person is about. The labels are too perfect to ignore, and very informative! Each person is very validated through these descriptions and we love connecting to them and honoring them in this way as well.

In times past, through my landline phone, I would often receive pre-recorded messages for the individual who previously had my phone number—even after a year. Without exception, each message was distinctly for me, and came with comforting words that I needed to hear at that time. While not working for many months, the message would be "Your unemployment check is on its way!" It was then that I knew I would be taken care of. And when needing a long rest after countless years of service, I would hear, "This is the Veteran's Hospital verifying your appointment." When I was in the midst of re-financing my home and not sure if I should pursue it again if declined, sure enough, a recorded message soon arrived saying, "This is your last chance to re-finance!"

Road signs continually give us messages and let us know that we are being acknowledged and spoken to from above. A woman I recently met sustained a terrible loss with the death of her teen-age son—a loss I cannot imagine enduring. Still in a state of grief after about two years, she cried out as she was driving one day, "Where are you?!! Where are you?!!" hoping to find comfort in perhaps knowing where her son was now. She suddenly noticed a road sign which read, "He is gone. He has risen."

Almost like having a conversation with an unseen force, when we ask, a response will always arrive which validates our situation and lets us know that we are not alone. And asking while driving almost always brings with it an answer in the form of a road sign, a license plate, or other written message along the way. When I could not decide if I should sell my home, I was pondering out loud when I came to a stop behind a large truck with huge letters painted on the back which read "MOVING?" And the very next car in from of me was an SUV with a bumper sticker which read, "Flip Floppin'."

Brokenhearted after my father's death, I went on a short road trip to get away. I found myself on the "Purple Heart Highway," which perfectly fit my life circumstances at that time. Unable to receive any of his personal effects as the circumstances surrounding his passing had prohibited me from having interaction with remaining family, I had lamented to myself one day, "If only I had one of his white handkerchiefs." For as long as I could remember, he carried a white handkerchief in his pocket...a symbol to me of his own personal energy. Shortly thereafter, I received a single white handkerchief from a group of my readers across the globe. And yet another reader sent a lovely pin to wear as an indicator of a grieving soul. On the back of the description paper it was attached to, was also this sentence near the copyright: "To Charles, Who was and is, My precious gift, My heart." My father's name was Charles. At their soul levels, my readers had heard my grieving and responded in kind. These were two of the very few responses I received during this time, but both were sent with a perfect and loving validation, assuring me I was being witnessed by a loving force from above. And when the challenge of grieving alone became more difficult than imagined, I received a "wrong number" text message that simply said, "how ya doin?"

This ever-present loving energy is always with us if we choose to see it. The more we evolve and are able to see what is outside of ourselves, thereby placing us outside of our self-imposed boxes of separation, the more we will come to know that we are not alone, as God and the universe are acknowledging and speaking to us every moment of every day. So even though the inhabitants of this planet may not be ready to acknowledge each other quite yet, God's energy is always ready and providing this experience for us. We are indeed loved, cared for, and being acknowledged from the unseen forces that permeate our very existence.

Signs of Direction

When I knew my prior path of assisting the planet was indeed over, the question of what to do next was frequently in the back of my mind. I was not sure what I would do next, as things had not quite settled out yet on the planet and the road was not yet clear. During a visit to North Carolina in 2010, while in a state of disconnect during my "in-between," out of the blue my granddaughter insisted I have lunch with her at her school. She was adamant. While at her school, my grandson's teacher suddenly approached me and begged me to give a presentation to the class. She did not care what it was about, "Just anything, but please come and speak to us the next time you are here." It was a bolt of lightning out of the blue, and I knew it had some kind of meaning. No one had "seen" me or connected to me for several months, and her invitation did not resemble my normal experience of late. Even with this message from a first-grade teacher, the entire message did not sink in, as I was still in shock from all the losses and not paying attention. But I did know that this was an invitation from the universe—I could feel it and see it.

Within days after returning home to New Mexico, it became clear that I needed to sell my home (my new neighbor had suddenly made his entrance!). I did not know where to move next. My daughter and grandchildren were very ready to leave North Carolina, so moving there never entered my mind. One night while watching television (I still watched television back then), a show came on about two clothing designers who traveled the US making special clothing for people with special circumstances. It was a great show—I loved the small and obscure places they visited all around the US and I soon remarked to myself, "I wish that show would come on again, and wherever they travel to this time is where I will move." The show did indeed come on once again, immediately after the prior one ended, and this time they arrived in a town in North Carolina, a short distance away from where my daughter and grandchildren lived. I could only laugh.

Another indicator that can assist us when we are deciding where to relocate, is to wait for an invitation from anyone or anything. In this way, God is speaking to us, as our energies combine. I knew my grandson's teacher was extending just that, and combined with the message from the television show, my new course was soon set. And as many of us know, once a good decision is eventually made, everything soon begins to snowball. But little did I know that it was not only the location that was calling me, but the children as well.

Our Personal Subconscious Guidance Systems

When we are going through massive transition and in the tunnel, or birth canal, it can be difficult to connect to ourselves in the ways we have been accustomed. We are losing our old selves, much of our ego selves, have been blocked from moving forward and re-creating the old and familiar, and in this way may find ourselves with a continual feeling of being lost and confused, as nothing feels remotely normal. We may not know who we are or where we are, making it difficult to make decisions. We may wake up each morning wondering where we are, even though it is clear that we are indeed in our bedrooms. When this occurs, we can always depend upon our personal subconscious guidance systems, as our subconscious is always clear and connected, even though our conscious selves may not be.

Linda had been with her partner for several years. They had a young son and Linda was now yearning for a daughter. Linda's partner had not treated her well over the years, but she continued to stay with him. Eventually, she decided it was time that they marry. Due to certain circumstances, they decided to marry openly with all the bells and whistles, but privately, they did not marry legally. Linda's subconscious self was telling her not to marry her partner. Deep down, she did not want to be with him, so she set up a "pseudo" marriage. And then there is Melinda, who suddenly found herself signing documents with her maiden name quite "accidentally."

Jeff kept driving away for the day, leaving his garage door wide open. He did this countless times. His subconscious was telling him to open the house up for a new occupant. And during that time, he continued to lose his house key as well. Subconsciously, he was no longer attached to his house. It was time for him to move.

Our bodies and personal energy know more than we do as well. When Janie met a man who eventually became her partner, she felt discombobulated whenever in his presence. Many times, she felt "off," stuttered and stammered around him, tripped and fell, could not find the right thing to wear, felt strangely insecure and insignificant, gained weight, was continually sick, they had awkward hugs, and she found it difficult to explain things to him. Her social skills also seemed to go out the window. "Are you always a fumbler-bumbler?" her mother asked one day. "No!" was her immediate reply. Although she and her partner had good times as well, their partnership was very short-lived as she had entered into it for spiritual reasons— all the while, her subconscious self was telling her

111

they were a terrible match. When we find ourselves fumbling and bumbling with no flow, it is a sign that two energies are a very poor fit. Finding just the right person creates the opposite. Things flow, we feel understood, we open up and can completely be ourselves, we relax, and we feel safe and at one with the other individual.

Our subconscious minds will also allow us to continually forget things and people with whom we do not wish to connect. But we will miraculously remember the most remote details of things we are in alignment with and with which we deeply want to connect. We can forget phone numbers, names of people and places, and much of anything else, but if our subconscious knows we are meant to connect with certain things, we will remember with great detail and in an uncanny way, certain things that are meant to stay with us. And like an idiot savant, our soul purpose as well, turns us into a sudden genius while bringing an intricate knowing and awareness of just what we are here to deliver.

We may get sick right before an important engagement, or find that we continually become ill whenever around certain people or places. Oops! Our subconscious is telling us these things are not a good fit. We may get severe allergic reactions while sitting in an audience or attending a seminar. Oops! Not a good fit. We may have a sneezing fit while at a specific location. Our subconscious is rejecting where we are. We may have a strange panic attack while in a new store or around a new group of people. Oops! This is not where we truly want or are meant to be. We may become tired or bored at specific times. No energy? Our subconscious is telling us we are not into it. We may become very angry when placed in certain situations, with a strong desire to get out as we feel trapped and used. Our subconscious is telling us that we absolutely do not want to be there. We may get lost trying to find a specific location. Our subconscious knows it is not a good place for us and will not allow us to connect. We may try to open a door at an establishment and find it is stuck. Oops! Not a good idea to enter.

We may gravitate to certain stores, places, people, or even works of literature and not know why. We simply feel good there and crave the energy. When I was re-connecting once again, I watched countless movies and read countless books that took place in the 1800's and early 1900's— and most of them took place in England. I was craving the days when a respectful presence and interaction between individuals was the norm. Bowing, nodding , and curtseying in acknowledgement of others was prominent in these films, and brought me great comfort as seeing souls acknowledging and respecting each other felt so right and true for me. I also loved the lack of internet, telephone, television, radio, or other methods of connection as I no longer had nor desired these myself. These films involved face-to-face connection with a true involvement with life, and the beauty of nature and the earth was always present as well. I had to watch myself though, as I began to get an English accent and tell others "I must take my leave" when it was time for me to go!

We naturally crave things we are meant to connect to. We may find ourselves watching a television interview more than once and not consciously know why, as there may be a trait in the person being interviewed that we need or want to adopt in ourselves. Our subconscious is guiding us there through a strong urge to connect for seeming unknown reasons. We may become obsessed with a place or activity, and it may simply be because it will lead us to where we need to be next on our journey. We may desperately desire to meet certain individuals, and find that it is only because we want to develop their traits within ourselves, as we have them but have yet to have utilized them. We are only seeing ourselves or at least our potential.

When watching a movie, what do you notice the most? Is it the nature and scenery, the plot, the characters, or perhaps the message? Each movie, story, or book we read always has a message for us if we choose to look for it. And usually, these messages are telling us where we are at that particular moment in our lives, and with greater clarity than we can muster up on our own. In addition, a movie may just have the information we have been seeking in resolution to a particular dilemma—God and the universe is answering, as always. Along with specific messages, movies and books can also attract our attention as they contain things that we gravitate to. So in this way, they are wonderful indicators of what we are holding in our hearts at that time.

Lyrics to songs can be great signs of guidance as well, along with bringing great comfort. We may suddenly, very out of the blue, find ourselves singing a song we had not heard for many years. The lyrics are bringing a message to us, as they are telling us where we are or even what we may need to know at that time. One of my personal favorites that pops in from time to time is *Counting Your Blessings* by Bing Crosby from one of my favorite movies, *White Christmas*.

When I'm worried and I can't sleep,
I count my blessings instead of sheep,
And I fall asleep counting my blessings.

It seems to pop in out of nowhere at times, and is a great reminder to focus on all that I have instead of all that I have lost. So many wonderful things are here for us if we remember to pay attention to what is right in front of us.

Have you been taking many vacations lately? Have you found that you seem to be gone more than you are here, or at least that your vacations are occurring with more frequency and lasting longer and longer? This is an indication that you may be ready for a *permanent* vacation, and the End Times eventually dictate a *total* vacation.

Our subconscious minds will always lead the way with an undeterred fervor, as they know with certainty what is best, right, and true for us at any given moment.

Signs from the Departed

There are times along the way when we receive messages from our loved ones who have parted through the physical death process, and with so many souls departing during the End Times, we are as always, all in this together and helping each other along the way.

I have been blessed with an ability to speak directly with souls who have crossed over through the death process, but receiving guidance and signs from departed souls through messages in our lives, has a completely different significance than speaking to them directly. Strangely enough, it is much more powerful, meaningful, and heartfelt than simply having a conversation with them. When we are in severe distress or even in unusual and immense joy and happiness, a beacon of energy is emitted, and our departed loved ones receive it. In this way, they may come to join us during times of crisis as well as during times of great happiness. So even through times of physical separation, we are always connected. And with the veil so thin now, we are closer than ever before.

One evening while still in the midst of processing the loss of my father, I was reading a novel with an uncanny resemblance to me. The heroine drove the same vehicle I did, and her life resembled mine in so many ways it became humorous. In addition, she was at the same place in her life that I was. This phenomenon happened with virtually every book I randomly selected from the library (even though I had no idea what the intricacies within the story would be), so over time, I had become accustomed to it. Mid-way through the book the words to a Methodist hymn were displayed across the page, and the composer of this hymn was a man named Charles Wesley. Not paying attention, I continued to read and then it hit me. My father's first name and middle names were Charles Wesley, and his parents were Methodist missionaries. Returning to the verse, I found a new comfort:

Jesus, lover of my soul, Let me to thy bosom fly,
While the nearer waters roll, while the tempest still is high,
Hide me, O my savior, hide, 'Til the storm of life is past;
Safe into the haven guide, O receive my soul at last!

Other refuge have I none, Hangs my helpless soul on thee,
Leave, O leave me not alone, Still support and comfort me.
All my trust on thee is stayed, All my help from thee I bring;
Cover my defenseless head, With the shadow of thy wing.

I had not been paying attention and had nearly missed a beautiful message connected to my father. Very indicative and descriptive of the present times, this hymn now brings me great comfort…especially as I know it was connected to much love…the love of my father. Another time, I was walking home from town and daydreaming. "Wouldn't it be nice," I thought, "if my father was walking toward me right now." Picturing him far down the sidewalk, with his tan shoes, glasses case in hand, and his familiar stride, he began to approach me as he walked ever so slowly, as I continued to walk toward him. Knowing well that when we met he would rearrange his feet with a little jump, making sure he was walking on the street side (as he had done so many, many times in our lives), I could just *feel* him there with me. At the point of our "meeting," I looked to my left and saw a very prominent sign at arm's length: *Charles Wesley House*. What comfort it brought! I have met many people over the years who desperately want to connect to a departed loved-one. I always ask them, "Did you ask for a sign?" and they most always say, "Yes! But nothing arrived!" Paying attention is the key to receiving signs. Many times, they are right in front of us, just waiting for us to acknowledge them, but for whatever reasons, we look right past them.

As the earth is being reborn, nothing seems normal anymore. We have literally been placed onto a very new grid. It can feel very strange indeed, as we have never been to this place before. We need to adjust then, to a new way of living and being, and connecting to the love-filled energy of God that permeates our existence every moment of every day, is an integral part of the new world reality.

With so much feeling strange and unfamiliar, and not much to connect to in the beginning stages, this time can be most challenging for those who are unusually sensitive. For these souls, they need a different path and different guidelines. Kindly read on for a glimpse into the life, challenges, and many gifts of the highly sensitive.

7

THE HIGHLY SENSITIVE PERSON

"DON'T TAKE THINGS SO personally!' "You're too sensitive!" "Everything is such a big deal to you!" "You need to develop a thick outer shell—you're too vulnerable." "You're so weak and fragile! Toughen up!" "Why can't you take things in stride?" If you have ever heard any of these words and phrases directed at you, you are most likely a highly sensitive person. And being a highly sensitive person on Planet Earth can at times, be quite a challenge, especially during the End Times.

Two women are wonderful experts on this subject and I would highly recommend their writings. *Making Work Work for the Highly Sensitive Person* by Barrie Jaeger, Ph.D. and *The Highly Sensitive Person* by Elaine N. Aron, Ph.D. If you are a highly sensitive person, you will most likely find yourself within the pages of these books.

Highly sensitive people (or HSPs), have a different experience with life than most individuals, as they are a very different breed altogether. And with their heightened sensitivities comes a challenge as well, as the earth does not remotely resemble what an environment should look like in their heart of hearts. In this way, it can be very helpful if these individuals develop a specific lifestyle that supports who they are and how they operate if they are to function well on the earth.

HSPs have special gifts. They sense what others do not and are able to pick up small and subtle energies that the majority of the population does not notice. So even though life can at times be a challenge for these individuals, if they enhance who they are and rely on their gifts, there can be many positive aspects to being here as well.

Very advanced souls, HSPs have had many experiences in the cosmos where everyone is wired as they are—this is what they know and are accustomed to, if even at subconscious levels. So in this way, they may not feel nearly at home here, as they may not understand why others seem overly harsh, thick-skinned, insensitive, and aggressive with their own personal agendas. The afore-mentioned traits are what seemed to work well in the old world; a world managed for so long by more aggressive energies embodying the old masculine energy. So take heart, sensitive souls, as the new world will eventually come to resemble a place that will finally feel like home—embodying a more gentle, feminine energy with heart at its core.

Easily tapped in and connected to a higher energy, HSPs usually embody a very natural spiritual sense. And because they are many times able to see and connect to energies that most others cannot sense, they usually have a strong and continual channel to another dimension altogether. Being a highly sensitive person myself, and having loved ones, acquaintances, and many readers who are also highly sensitive, a chapter devoted to these souls is most certainly warranted during the End Times.

Below are some common traits of a highly sensitive person (and know as well, that there are always exceptions and variations to any of these traits):

- *We become easily overwhelmed.* HSPs become over-stimulated easily. We pick up so much at any given time, that when too much is going on, it can feel like too much energy is bombarding us all at once. Generally speaking, small things to an HSP are like big things, as our heightened sensitivities cannot accept outside stimulation like most others can. So in this way, HSPs become overwhelmed very easily as little things feel like big things and too many things are simply far too many things!

- *We are more emotional and passionate than most.* HSPs *feel* much more than an average person does, and because of this, we can be much more emotional than most people are. We may tear up more frequently, upset more easily, find it difficult to witness pain in others (usually running at the sight of blood!), and feel the situations of others more than they do themselves. HSPs also laugh easily and can change moods very rapidly.

- *We take things more personally.* This is not about having too much of our ego selves, resulting in taking things personally, but about feeling things so much that we take things to heart. In addition, when things on the planet do not remotely resemble the higher ways of love, respect, and caring, sensitive souls feel very wounded at deep levels when experiencing the lower vibrating actions of others. It is really about a heart wound and a sadness of planetary and human conditions. We feel wounded for the planet and not necessarily for ourselves.

- *We experience panic and anxiety more frequently than others do.* HSPs are very fearful of being overwhelmed. So whether consciously or subconsciously, we may feel panic when in certain situations, as we know we may likely become overwhelmed. A fear of becoming overwhelmed and over-stimulated causes the panic— not necessarily the overstimulation itself (which is distressing all on its own). Anxiety also occurs when the outer world of an HSP does not resemble his/her inner world, or the world we know in our heart of hearts. We will then feel lost and ungrounded in unfamiliar territory, and when finding ourselves in lower vibrating energies, feeling panic is simply a good barometer indicating that we do not belong there.

- *We tire easily.* Because we are so sensitive, HSPs tire easily and need more rest than most. And many times, we have a need to eat frequently as we experience blood sugar swings if we exert too much.

- *We need "less" than most others do.* Lower doses of medication, lower volume of sound, softer aromas or none at all, less stimulation around us, softer visuals, less hot weather, less cold weather, and the like are what we prefer. Harsh in regard to most anything does not sit well with an HSP. For some of us, our bodies respond very differently to things than a "normal" body does—we are simply a different breed altogether (my body temperature has been a continual 93° for my entire life, and no health practitioner seem to know why!).

- *We do not like crowds.* Again, we can become overwhelmed and over-stimulated by too much energy in one spot. We may be able to tolerate crowds and over-stimulations for short periods, but an HSP will shortly find him/herself craving a time out in due time.

- *We do not easily adjust to change.* HSPs can easily be thrown off-balance because of our heightened sensitivities to our environment. Movement and the unfamiliar can very easily knock us out of our grooves and we lose our footing. Our stronger connection is to the unseen world, so in this way, we are not always as grounded as others are.

- *We shy away from managing a lot.* A dominant posture is too aggressive for an HSP, and we are not then, comfortable telling people or things what to do. Taking into consideration the needs and feelings of others (almost to a much greater degree than necessary), we may fear oppressing another. Generally speaking, we do not like to be forceful.

- *We are very connected to nature.* Very sensitive to our environment, HSPs love the nature spirits and the natural world as it more closely resembles our memories and connection to a more highly evolved world and reality. And the energies of nature more closely resemble our own as well.

- *We may consider the needs of others more than our own.* This can be a downfall for HSPs, as we may be overly sensitive to others, and completely neglect our own personal needs and desires.

- *We like to stay home.* HSPs frequently prefer their own personal environment. We know what to expect there, have created our environment to suit our needs and who we are, and are thus surrounded by energies that feel good to us. In other words, we need our own personal sanctuaries in order to stay sane.

- *We enjoy our alone time more than most.* In order to recharge and rejuvenate, an HSP prefers to gather and recoup his/her energy by being alone rather than taking from an outside source. Being alone also provides a protection from over-stimulation and creates a restful respite.

- *We may not prefer a "busy" life-style.* Less is more for an HSP. Being too busy over-stimulates us and many times we prefer simplicity, which enables us to experience a more pure, connected, and meaningful life.

- *We need and must have more calm around us than others do.* HSPs can wear out more easily than others can when having stimulation or moving energy around them for long periods. In this way, HSPs do not do well living on busy streets, near construction sites, being in the company of highly energized people for long periods, or even in environments when continued movement and commotion are present.

- *Many HSPs have psychic or unusual abilities.* Because HSPs are so highly sensitive, many of us are able to tap into the unseen world with relative ease if we so choose. We sense energies around us that go unnoticed by others and may also have an uncanny ability to know when something is about to happen.

- *We can spot another HSP a mile away.* When another HSP is in the near vicinity, it is as if we have come home, found an easy connection, and family is now at our fingertips. And because HSPs are so sensitive to the needs and feelings of others, having another HSP as a friend is usually a great experience.

- *We are usually very considerate.* Because of our unusual sensitivities, HSPs are overly thoughtful of the needs of others. We are generally very respectful, good listeners, very aware of what is going on with those around us, and care deeply about our loved ones. For us, we are all one, and we remember well that this is indeed so.

- *We are highly creative.* HSPs can easily tap into outside energies (making us natural channels), allowing us to be very artistic with a love and ability with music, art, gardening, writing, cooking, and the like, and we are many times multi-talented as well.

126

- *We hold a vision of the way things are in more evolved places.* Natural visionaries, HSPs hold an innate blueprint and comfort zone of a more highly evolved way of living and being, whether consciously or not.

- *We are very cooperative.* Understanding the needs of the whole, HSPs tend to be sensitive to their environments along with embodying a higher blueprint of group interaction. We very naturally conform to the wishes of others and are supportive of what another is bringing forth or trying to accomplish. This can at times be a downfall as well, as we may not speak up when we need to.

HSPs have had a bad rap for many years, as we can appear to be weak, fragile, and even ineffective (and at times, we certainly can be). We do not tend to take on a lot, so career wise, we are rarely found in positions of great authority and management, nor in the public eye where we must have a tough outer shell. It is common for an HSP to be more comfortable in a job that is far beneath his/her levels of being, purpose, and abilities, as there is less stimulation there and much more ease and simplicity. And in addition, with so much of the old world now a bad fit for us, a "normal" job will rarely find its way to our door. We would most likely be miserable there, as it would not remotely resemble what we have now become. But as we progress on our personal evolutionary path, we can come to know that we eventually find spaces and situations that fit most perfectly with whom we are and how we operate best.

In regard to a career or generating an income, HSPs tend to work well at home. This allows us the space we need, a control on outside stimulation, and the freedom to take frequent breaks or diversions if needed. Being self-employed is another good fit for an HSP, as creativity is on-going in many aspects of work or calling, as is freedom and flexibility. In addition, we can tailor our work or calling to fit more precisely who we are and how we thrive.

Most HSPs do not fare well with a mandatory 40-hour workweek, or enclosed in a building with a harsh or sterile environment with designated break times. This kind of regimen is very contrary to whom and what we are about, and will greatly serve to shut us down, make us depressed, and most certainly exhaust us. But as we evolve through this evolutionary process, we begin to fine-tune these things. As so much that no longer fits us begins to fall away, what remains is most always a perfect fit for what we need in order to thrive and become passionate again.

Honoring our own personal needs is vitally important as well. HSPs need to take care of themselves more than most people do. Self-care, time-outs, and allowing for our own personal needs above the needs of others is crucial if we are to remain happy, centered, grounded, and our best selves. Many times, even a short break of half an hour is enough to restore us and will allow us to be up and going with a new and fresh energy. But if we are overly exhausted, we may even need several days to restore and if we are very drained and depleted, several months. Asking for what we need in all areas of our lives, there-by placing ourselves first and tending to ourselves, greatly enhances our states of being and supports who and what we are all about.

HSPs need to be rested more than most others do. When sleep deprived or worn out, we can experience panic, foggy thinking, feel as if we are not all here, and feel ineffective and powerless. And making sure our serotonin levels are up is very important as well if we wish to be at our best. The two "S" s, sleep and serotonin, are vitally important for an HSP.

In general, having the freedom to tailor our work, lives, and environment to fit our own personal needs and desires makes for a happy and thriving HSP (and for any other person as well!). We will be more productive, more creative, more centered, more rested, and much more pleasant to be around.

HSPs and the End Times

With so many heightened sensitivities, HSPs pick up on the unseen energies of the End Times more than most others do. Even if there is nothing occurring on the planet that has made itself visible, an HSP will know and sense that monumental things are occurring nonetheless. HSPs will simply *feel* tremendous amounts of energy falling away, departing, unraveling, and making a mass exit. In this way, many of us will feel highly ungrounded, lost, scattered, insecure, and feel that we are in a space grossly unfamiliar that makes no sense to us. These are general and continuous feelings that will persist for many months, as the End Times are not a short and sweet occurrence. Things simply feel strange and weird, creating continual feelings of unfamiliarity and bewilderment, as if we are now in a strange land that exists in a strange time warp or burp in the cosmos. (Know as well, that if you *are not* an HSP, but very connected to your soul path, you will feel these things as well. HSPs may feel them to a degree that their lives are affected and it may become difficult to function at normal levels.)

One thing that can help to greatly ease the "un-ease," is remembering that we are always taken care of during these rare and unprecedented times. We are continually being watched over and monitored, guided, molded, and navigated towards spaces of ease and comfort that fit who and what we are all about at any given moment. In this way, we can rest assured that all is always well, even though we are sensing what appears to be otherwise.

Another great remedy for these challenging feelings is creating a distraction and an escape. Finding an outlet connected to our passions and spending time and focus on that, greatly assists in taking us to a different space, at least for a while. The planet is going to make its changes no matter where we are and what we do, and because many of us have been released from our prior duties of assisting with the transition, an escape then, is certainly appropriate during this time.

The earth changes can create additional challenges for HSPs. Each time a tornado comes near our area, I can feel the massive energy it creates for a few days before and after. Even though these tornadoes always pass around us, feeling their intense energy always throws me for a loop. Intense solstice energy will do the same for me, and at times, it can take weeks for me to get back on track. As these cleansings and earth movements are coming at rapid rates now, these are situations that we will need to become accustomed to, more than ever before. Relaxing remedies can greatly assist with these strong energy movements. A relaxed system more easily allows these energies to move through us, and staying calm assists as well (flower remedies and the like can be very beneficial).

The movements of the planets can also be felt intensely by HSPs. These planetary movements serve a different purpose than the earth changes. Our beloved celestial bodies each contain their own specific energies with their own specific blueprint or purpose. So in this way, the planets are here to assist and to serve us during the End Times. They bring in new energy that is needed at the time, and going with their flow greatly helps us to be in alignment with the divine plan, bringing more ease for us in all ways.

During times of great movement, an HSP can become easily overwhelmed. Whether with invisible energies or with very real experiences around us, constant disruption occurs when these massive movements occur. If at all possible, it can greatly help to have a simple life with lots of room for flexibility and time outs. Anything that promotes calm in us, is of course, always helpful, whether it be a calm friend to spend time with, calming herbs, deep breathing, yoga, hugging a tree (or a human!), or even relaxing music. Spending time in beautiful surroundings with nature all around, can bring a much needed calm and grounding as well. And of course, being with the children as much as possible is the best remedy for any upset that I know of. The children have such an amazing energy, that we can be taken to new spaces altogether in a matter of minutes.

The New HSPs…the Children

Many of our new little ones are highly sensitive. They hold the new energy of the new world in all ways and it can be a joy to be in their presence. Although they have heightened sensitivities, they also embody tremendous strength as well. And this is a combination that has been lacking in many HSPs until now. Yes, we HSPs are very strong indeed—this is not what I am referring to. The new children embody a beautiful balance of sensitivity combined with great power and unwavering strength. They do not have the vulnerabilities that most HSPs do. They are rarely perceived as weak and fragile, have a stability and grounding that is intense, a forceful nature, and a confidence that goes unsurpassed even though they are highly sensitive souls as well.

Our new little ones embody a forceful and aggressive posture because that is what is needed with the creation of the new world. They know exactly what they are doing, and will unwaveringly do it well. With high energy, as they hold so much of it, they are like lasers who go directly for what they want. They are a force to be reckoned with. And even with all this forceful energy (which they embody so as not to be swayed), they still maintain their sensitive natures.

Very cooperative and tuned to assisting others, they embody many traits of an HSP as well. They love nature, music, art, are tapped into the unseen world, can communicate telepathically with ease, and know the energy of love exceedingly well. Again, their main difference is that they are

132

not easily bowled over and can be forceful and aggressive, as they know that they are here to bring a new world into existence, and to bring the new energy into existence as well. "Don't mess with me!" they seem to say. "I know exactly what I am doing and I am now in charge!" And just as quickly, they can move to calm, sweetness, sensitivity and love, changing moods and personal energy as quickly as any HSP. Very mature for such little ones, they have an ability to monitor themselves when needed. And of course, our newest little ones use the energy of love and the heart to conquer all. The new children are our greatest asset and our greatest teachers. We are so blessed to have them here at this time— they are holding the space well.

So now we have released and let go of much, whether highly sensitive or not. What next? Will our emptiness finally be filled with something new, or do we sit with an empty shell feeling hollow and not all here for an immeasurable period of time? There is indeed a method to the madness of all the losses, and it culminates with the arrival of the predominant energy of the new world—the heart.

8

THE HEART ENERGY FINALLY ARRIVES

EMPTYING OUT, EMPTYING OUT, emptying out. We are indeed empting out and letting go of anything and everything that does not fit the energy of the new world. We lose much of our old lives and our old selves, and many of our loved ones as well. After all these losses, this phase of our spiritual evolutionary process is still not complete, believe it or not—because after we are as empty as we can imagine a soul can be, we usually experience a final cleansing.

Very spontaneous and as if on cue from a higher power beyond ourselves, our bodies will frequently undergo a massive cleanse in order to make us as squeaky clean as possible. I have always loved this aspect of our spiritual evolutionary process—the fact that it simply does what is needed all on its own. In this way, we can get out of the way and allow a much higher power to take over and assist us in this process—and most of the time, as always, what is needed is rarely our own idea.

Because we have emptied out so much in prior months, we may have a strong desire to satisfy ourselves in some way, but nothing ever seems to do the trick. We may crave a certain food and think, "A good piece of pie would be a nice treat and make me feel better," or even "I'm just going to relax and watch a good movie." Or perhaps, "I think I will take a walk in nature, as that will surely help. I know! — an art class or maybe a dance class. Hmmm…a cold beer and a good book?" We are hungry, but for what we do not know, as nothing seems to fit this strange and deep hunger within us. Because we are so very empty, and what we are really craving is more heart and love in our space, our old remedies for giving us a brief satisfaction no longer work. So during this time of great emptiness, we must simply accept the fact that we feel empty…period. There is no remedy in sight until we are quite empty enough for the heart energy to fill us up once again.

A final cleanse (and nothing is ever final, but this one takes the cake for at least a while) constitutes a final clearing out in order to allow us to accept the heart energy more fully. So even though we may have been removed from much already, which has allowed us to begin to "see" things more clearly, we will really begin to see more clearly after our physical body cleanse.

The planet is of course undergoing her cleanse as well in the form of climatic events such as flooding, hurricanes, fire, and tornadoes, so in this way, because residing here automatically makes us microcosms for the planet, we are undergoing personal massive cleansings as well.

Rashes, acne, skin eruptions, coughing and congestion, urinary tract problems, and our old friend the intestinal distress are common symptoms of body cleansing. Sweating, nausea, great changes in appetite and food preference, and other ways of releasing toxins are also prevalent during a cleansing. And as always, it is best to consult a health care professional to make sure there is nothing more serious occurring, as all our strange symptoms are not always attributable to the ascension process.

During an ascension cleanse, our immune systems go on hyper-alert, so in this way, we can reject much that we put into our bodies. Through it all, we may eventually come to a point where we can only accept pure foods and beverages, along with any other things pure on the planet. We may also find ourselves reverting to the days before everything became contaminated. Listening to music we have not listened to for many years, taking up fitness practices and/or taking care of ourselves like we used to, going back to old and more pure spiritual energies as well, and generally finding ourselves in spaces that felt good in times past, are manifestations of this stage. We are without a doubt being fine-tuned to accept the best, and this includes the heart energy.

What is producing this final cleanse and why is it any different from prior cleansings that many of us experienced up until now? Because we have come so far and are now in a very new space in the cosmos, the earth is now turning inside out, or what I frequently refer to as "doing a somersault." She must fit her new space in all ways. In a quite amazing way, she is being reborn, just as we are being reborn right along with her. Down she goes to the depths of "the bottom," only to begin a very new rise upwards once again. This nosedive creates a great purging or digging out of the lower energies from every nook and cranny existing on the earth. As the new earth reaches downward, the earth and the new light grasp what is there and pull it out—in order to be released or in order to be more visible so love and the heart energy can find it. This is quite different from the purging and releasing done in the past, as layers and layers were being released during that time. We have indeed made so much progress from releasing so many layers, that we are at the tail end of the releasing, which is why... we are experiencing the arrival of the heart energy and why the earth is now turning itself inside out.

With so much being usurped and disrupted from its hiding place during the somersault phase and beyond, it is then do or die—everything must embody the heart energy or depart. Many souls are leaving the planet at this time for this very reason. They either came while the old world was in existence, and have no interest in living in the new world, they cannot make the needed internal changes, or they simply do not wish to be here during the massive transition. There are several other symptoms of the earth's somersault phase. The most common are listed below:

- *Boundary issues.* Because so much is moving at an intense pace now, and we are in "the somersault," anything and everything can now arrive in our spaces— and some things that arrive can be most unpleasant. Insect and human invasions are on this list as well. But other things are quite lovely. In this way, we may suddenly feel vulnerable for no reason, or at times, for very good reason! But again, there are also things arriving in our spaces that we feel grateful for, as more light has finally arrived at last.

- *Halloween is here all year.* Part of the purging and movement involves darker energies flying around, as they have been dislodged. We may find that somehow we end up watching a scary or unpleasant movie when not the norm for us, or the like. Or we may simply feel spooked for no apparent reason, and even have bad dreams and nightmares.

- *We cannot keep up with our lives.* So much energy is moving right now, along with our movement into higher vibrating territory, that we soon find we are manifesting too quickly to keep up. Think of something and it shows up almost instantly. Add to this the purging of the old and denser energies, and there is a lot going on. In this way, we may feel that we are never able to stay on top of things, or get much of anything under control before something new arrives that needs our attention. *Everything* is being moved into a new space, and can we ever feel it!

- *Things never seem to complete.* Similar to above, except that we are moving so quickly now, that we may begin something, and very soon it no longer fits where we are as we have already evolved out of that space—or, the space we were moving toward has evolved as well and no longer exists. So we may move into new territory, take the first few steps, and find that we cannot go any further. The energies are moving things into very new spaces at a rapid rate. In this way, much is upside down, inside out, here and there, and hard to grab onto. In addition, what we may have begun may suddenly no longer apply. All of this creates "half done."

• *Emotional symptoms as well!* A common feeling during the End Times is the hysteria energy. For unidentifiable reasons, we may feel a subtle underlying hysteria as so much is moving and changing, or even that we are hyperventilating. And as always, the usual panic, anxiety, and depression as well. There is too much change and overload, even at the unseen levels.

We may wake up one morning and find that a current passion we had recently been fostering, very suddenly has absolutely no interest for us. It is as if it has suddenly disappeared from our consciousness, never to return again. This is simply an indicator that a cleansing has most indeed taken affect as we more closely arrive at the destination of a very new reality where everything will begin fresh and clean —brand new.

We may find that we suddenly have a new and strange way of dressing—at least strange for us. For most of my life, I wore clothing that fit my residency in the Southwest—ready for a hike at any moment, with rugged shoes, hearty shirts, and strong jeans or shorts. I have never been a "dress" kind of girl. But suddenly I began wearing skirts, dresses, and dainty shoes! I even began painting my toenails. Yikes! And a very new hairstyle came along with it. As we turn inside out, we are then given an opportunity to balance out, or rather to experience things that existed in the "opposing" side of our reality, and this frequently has to do with the feminine energy. In addition, we may find ourselves eating a diet that is the complete and total opposite of what we have eaten and preferred for our entire lives—or perhaps even placing our right foot in our left shoe as we dress. Again, we are turning inside out, which now enables us to arrive at the opposite shore of our prior existence during this phase of our evolutionary journey. We are passing by new horizons as we balance out...just like the earth. And as the energy of the feminine begins to embrace us, as it greatly relates to the energy of the new world, this influence can be felt in many ways as well.

We may experience vivid and rocky dreams at night, with a continual restless sleep as much is turned inside out in the world around us (and within as well), as the cleanse and restructuring continue. And our dreams may just be plain strange, with anyone and anything within them. We may find that brief day naps bring us the peace we need, as the nights are simply too tumultuous. Food may become difficult to digest as our systems are now on overload with this massive "turning," and we may find that drinking liquids and eating mild is what we strangely crave.

We may find that the business world is simply too much for us now, as these ways of interacting in the rigid mental world and with money at the core simply throw us off, make us fumble and bumble with an inability to connect and communicate with others, and drain us at best. As business begins its *own* turning, there are still opportunities in regard to business with those who have service and heart at their core, so all is not always lost. Speaking the heart language and not the business language of times past is the key, and will at least allow us a bit more time until the massive changes are complete.

But slowly and surely, and in small and beautiful increments, as so much is cleansed and emptied out, the heart energy begins to fill us up. Stiff necks, pinched nerves, allergies, joint pain, foot stiffness and pain, and other strange maladies can arrive with it, but they become brief and inconsequential as the heart energy begins to take over. The heart energy is *pushing out* from a very new base, and removing everything in its path that does not resonate with or embody its energy. Expansion is ever present then, as this new and higher vibrating energy will soon comprise the air that we breathe. As we adjust then, to a new base, we frequently experience unexplained pain in our feet and lower extremities, as this expansion takes over at the bottom levels, slowly moving its way up and out in times to come.

As we begin to fill up with this energy comprised of heart and love, we also begin to operate in a different way as well. The second phase of our spiritual evolutionary process can make us feel downright strange the majority of the time. All we know is what we have always known in regard to what we have been accustomed to in times past. But now, things are beginning to be very different indeed. We have a new normal, and along with it, a new purpose as well, and add to this a massive loss of ego and "strange" may be an understatement. Nothing is the way it used to be, and trying to recapture it only places us back in spaces that will eventually be non-existent. In addition, we have been removed from much during this phase, and this fact in itself can serve as a comfort if we choose to see it that way—as we have been removed for our own protection, security, and ease. As always, we are being taken care of with great love.

Very soon, we may find ourselves having a new love, forgiveness, and tolerance for others, as it is not about separating and culling the higher energies from the lower energies now, but about love, caring, and deep respect. We may look around us and see a heaven on earth that we have never seen before. Nature is now ever so magnificent, even more than we had noticed in our entire lifetimes, and we may feel gratitude for many, many things as well. Goodness and love may appear to be everywhere, people are happier and friendlier, and we can now wake up and be thrilled and awed to be alive at this time. Problems iron themselves out in no time, as they become fewer and far between. And our atmosphere is magical most every day…simply magical. We may blink our eyes and wonder where in the world we are.

As many of us watch from the sidelines now, as the remainder of the planet makes its changes, we can watch with great love in our hearts. Interfering, helping, meddling, guiding, and creating too much new are now very much prohibited and completely out of alignment with where we are now meant to be. In this way, we now get to watch with love and understanding, as the many souls on the earth begin to recover themselves and find their way at last. There will of course, be those who never recover themselves, and these souls will eventually depart. As the recovering souls remember within what is most important, they will eventually find the souls who have "departed" while still here, see them once again, and a new world will then be ready for creation. All we need be about now, is simply the energy of the heart—our very new purpose. And during this time of watching and loving, all our needs will miraculously be met.

If we follow the mantras *Thank you God for everything* and *Everyone is always helping me*, we can come to know that no matter what things look like in times to come, a loving presence from above is monitoring and navigating the End Times in a beautiful and miraculous way, all with divine perfection. Budget cuts, a changing and tight economy, new airline provisions and constraints, unstable fuel prices, and bickering, stubborn, and insistent strange behavior from politicians, are all in divine order. At their soul levels, they are greatly assisting in bringing the new world to our fingertips at a rapid rate.

The thrust from above is all about going local. In this way, we can begin to connect to our brothers and sisters face to face, to see and acknowledge one another, and to respect and care about each other once again. So although it may appear that some are insistent in cutting funds at the national levels for much needed programs, along with education for our young ones (to give an example), these disastrous acts are supporting the planet in becoming an entity that is comprised of many smaller entities, or rather *local*. The same holds true for escalating gasoline prices for no apparent reason, acute restrictions and higher prices with airline travel, taxation, insurance, and the like. We are being forced to stay home and look at what is right in front of us. Part of turning inside out creates local, as it is the new format for the new world.

As each individual community begins to come together, acknowledging what it needs and feels is best for itself (due to the many changes imposed on our old ways), we will be forced to become localized. Local food distribution and farming, employment, health care facilities that are designed to meet the needs of each community's citizens, educational facilities, and the like, can then be tailored to be in alignment with the immediate surrounding energies and needs of its residents. Each local community can then make decisions of their own that perfectly fit who and what each community is about.

In times past, many souls on the planet became caught up in what was being presented to them, not looking far enough outside of themselves, and not remembering what was really and truly important—which is love and the heart energy. Internet in general began to lose its divine purpose, as in many ways it eventually became a home for lower energies. But this was in divine order as well. So even though pornography, social networking (instead of face to face connecting), a gross lack of privacy, along with great strides in hacking and duplicating the digital works of others (to give examples) took over, these changes will only serve to create the downfall of an old grid. (Remember, our evolutionary process dictates that as old structures are abandoned, the lower energies arrive and take over.) It is now time for a very new grid, and this grid will be comprised of the hearts and souls of the inhabitants of the earth as they interact directly with each other. In this way, as we evolve individually, we will no longer have a desire to connect to the internet or even to watch television, as we are now being tuned to connecting to each other at local levels and with each other face to face.

There will be communities that will come together and create wonderful things very far ahead of others, as each individual community will come up with new and innovative ways to self-sustain, all in alignment with the individual purpose and energy of each community. As other areas on the planet will be experiencing massive cleansings, as well as darker energies moving to the surface before they depart, some areas then, will be much more unpleasant to reside in than others. In this way, the communities that are far ahead and self-sustaining ,with a strong local support, respect, and caring, will be having their own individual experience, shut off and far removed from the remainder of the planet. But eventually, all communities will connect when there exists matching levels of vibration or evolution into the new. (Many areas receiving massive cleansings will rebuild in alignment with the energy of the new world, if they so choose, and in this way, these areas will hold the highest vibration of all.)

How did we finally get here after all the strife and struggle, and is this emerging new world going to stay, or is it simply another carrot dangly before our eager noses?

In summation of recent events in 2011: The divine powers from above finally ascertained that many souls currently on the planet were simply not waking up nor willing to embody enough light all on their own. In this way, the spiritual evolutionary plan began to move forward once again nonetheless—basically, without the "co-operation" of the souls here who continued to lag behind. As more light arrived from above instead of from within, earth changes and cleansings occurred to assist individuals and the planet in receiving as much light as possible—thus, emptying everything out, but receiving new light as well.

Before this crucial pivotal point of the death of the old and the emergence of the new, things were very different, but with good reason. Those who came to assist in raising the vibration of the planet, very diligently gave it their all as healers, speakers, teachers, artists, and the like. They needed to reach as many people as possible, and in this way, the internet (for example) was a vital tool utilized for this purpose. And offering services for little or no compensation was part of this way of being as well, as reaching as many souls as possible was the goal during this time. When this phase was over, it was over. The time was up. In this way, these loving and giving souls could now tend to themselves and no longer needed to reach out to many. They will focus on their individual local communities in times to come, and eventually connect to other individual communities— when the time is right—*and also*, if they so choose to leave their own individual heaven on earth and come out again at all.

There is no turning back now. We are on course once again and moving full speed ahead. Will we come together and hold hands in times to come, as was the original plan? Will we embody enough light within ourselves to form a new grid of light consisting of human beings full of love? And what if the inhabitants of the earth still insist on the same, refusing to look outside of themselves and refusing to create love and caring within themselves? Will this seeming hell on Earth remain forever? This is where experiencing all the losses comes into play once again. And this is, as well, when the heart energy takes over like an all-encompassing womb that wraps itself around us, with arms holding us in a loving embrace.

Again, the reason so much light from above did not arrive in the years immediately prior to 2011, was for very good reason. The divine powers wanted to give the inhabitants of the earth as much time as possible to embody this light within themselves, all on their own. It was time for the new grid of light consisting of the love of human beings to finally form. As mentioned many times within this book, this did not happen as hoped at that time. If the light began to arrive from above once again when the inhabitants of the earth were not yet ready, they would only use it to create self-indulgent lower vibrating creations, and the earth would hence, not progress into the planet of light that was intended. So in this way, the light was unable to arrive from above until the time was right.

So now, as we begin to move forward once again, we must stay on course if even perhaps in a different way than was originally planned. The planets are planning on assisting us in a great way in 2012, and we need to stay on course in order to utilize this great assistance offered to us in times to come. There will of course, be other planetary alignments that will arrive to assist us before 2012, as we are all in this transition together, supporting and helping each other in all ways.

Like a sailboat tacking on the ocean, hearts will open while light arrives. The many losses that will occur will serve to open the hearts of many, and this, in itself, will form a very new connection and bond. One cannot know what it is like to experience massive losses, unless they have experienced the same. These losses are vastly heart-opening. So in this way, these hearts will come together and form a heart connection and new grid comprised of the energy of the heart. And of course, our newest arrivals, the new babies, already embody this energy to a great degree.

As we have evolved out of "helping," we will soon find ourselves in the energy of the new world, which is about *partnership*. Helping indicates that one needs assistance, as they are not powerful within themselves and another knows more. *Partnership* dictates equal distribution, or more than one soul assisting another in rare times when needed. Giving is the same. *Sharing* is what will prevail in the new world, as one soul shares his/her gifts with another. Giving dictates a movement of energy out of one's field of center, and *sharing* dictates staying still and centered with equality between two parties, which is the more evolved energy of the new world. Thus, we will hold hands in equality while we form the new grid of the new world (and this is one of the many reasons, as well, why this book will be my last offering of this nature…my services are no longer needed.) Eventually, we will all be on equal turf with the new leveling that has taken place.

As our planet and new spaces evolve into the energy of love, we will find that somehow we have become a more graceful and subtle human being. We are now more gentle in all ways. In times past, or in the first phase of our spiritual evolutionary process, we needed to embody a more forceful energy within ourselves. Much energy needed to move and great change needed to occur. This required much more ego as well. This time is now over. We may now feel weak, ineffective, invisible, unable to make a decision, and unsure of much of everything. We may feel that we are no longer in charge of anything, and that we are most certainly no longer at any kind of helm. This is all rightfully so in the beginning stages of the second phase. We needed to be whittled down, beaten down, and removed of much, so that our old ego selves would now be out of the way. A loss of ego makes us still. It makes us more vulnerable and real. And most importantly, it creates a human being who is now very ready to accept the new energy of the heart, because ultimately, that is all that really exists that is remotely real. With every thought arising from our ego selves, whether it be a thought of self-criticism, fear, or misperceptions of a world that is not comprised of heart, arrives a massive heat wave within—all designated for the burning up of the ego. And as we have lost so much of our ego selves through this process, interacting with others becomes a very different experience as well.

When interacting with anything that does not speak "heart" (or rather if there is no heart at the core), our interactions can become discombobulated, confusing, flat, sad, and throw us off, making us feel more lost than ever. We may lose our confidence, feel insignificant, experience a wounded heart, and most always, we will short-circuit, as our energy cannot flow. We cannot relate in any way to what the other is talking about, to the life they are living, or how they operate. For us, a world and reality with heart at its core, is all there is. There is simply no connection then, as the heart energy is the only energy in the new world. Others do not "see" us, cannot hear us, and our interactions become puppet-like, as if we are acting in a strange play with our lines written by someone who does not remotely understand who we are and what we are about—as if others cannot see what is all around them, what is really and truly occurring, and why. They are in one world and we are in another.

As we eventually begin to connect to others, do we allow anyone and everyone in our spaces just because he or she knows about our spiritual evolutionary process? With this new love ever present, do we throw our doors open to anything and everything now? Very emphatically, *no...* we do not need to do this. We will very naturally connect to those who are residing in the same energetic spaces that we are, and to those who are now embodying as much heart energy as we are. We do not need to intentionally attempt to force a connection, as with like energies attracting like energies, we will connect all on our own when the time is right. Contrary to the saying, *We are all one*, we are indeed all one at very high levels of being, but until enough of the planet has lost much of its ego energy, this oneness does not need to occur unless all parties are willing and especially until all parties are ready. Saying "I am just like you!" and "We are all one!" is not necessarily true, just because many of us experience many of the same symptoms. We have a right to choose our own friends and those with whom we feel a good and pleasant connection. "With whom do I feel good around and feel my best self? Whose company do I enjoy the most? With whom am I the most me? Who am I with when I like myself the best? Who loves and cares about me the most?" are good questions we can ask ourselves when deciding whom to allow into our spaces. Many of us may be having many of the same experiences, but until we have lost a substantial part of our old selves and what remains for most of us is simply the heart energy, contrary connections are not always a good idea—

even if they come from a non-judgmental or more highly evolved self.

As the energy of the heart progresses on the planet, and much begins to fall away, what is left is what really matters. In this way, individual preferences to life style, entertainment, and personal choices will begin to lessen, as what remains will be common to us all. The relationships then, that remain intact or that form a-new, will all be based on the connecting force of love. Love is the glue that holds everything together in the new world, and much of anything else will feel flat, two-dimensional, and leave us feeling unfulfilled like an empty shell. And of course, will fall away all on its own, or at least be brought into the light for an opportunity to shift into a new format based on love. (But until we have reached a pivotal point during this phase, having good and healthy boundaries is still a good idea for most of us.)

When enough individuals on the planet reach a certain threshold, the heart energy will then take over and raise everyone and everything up, embracing our entire reality in its loving arms. Enough individuals will need to be at a point where they can "see" the love that is present, in order to embrace it, and this will occur after many losses and cleansings. Love is a changer and a healer—there is no disputing it.

I once had a partner who had a great dog. When I first met the dog, he was sad, sulked around with his head down, had frequent seizures, kidney problems, and arthritis. One day, he experienced a massive kidney dysfunction and I had to take him to the vet. The veterinarian said that he might not survive. He stayed on IV fluids for three days, and then I picked him up. Around that time, my partner left for several weeks for work related purposes. It was then just the two of us—this great dog and me—and what a wonderful time we had. I had never had a dog before, and had no idea what to do with him. We cuddled on the sofa every morning, we went on several walks each day, I took him everywhere with me in the car, and we talked, and talked, and talked. Eventually, I would find him lying on the floor outside of the shower when I bathed. He soon began to get a spring in his step, prancing around with his head held high, tail wagging, and with a smile on his face (yes, dogs do smile...I just know they do!). As our time together progressed, he began frolicking and chasing birds when we walked, jumping in the river, and he even began barking for the first time ever. He discontinued having seizures and health issues, which he had experienced for several years, and all was well. I will never forget our special time together. He turned into a very different dog in those few weeks—and I believe it was all due to love— the greatest changer and greatest healer. My partner said I was pampering him and turning him into a girl (okay...I did let him sleep next to me with his head on the other pillow...but it was only one time!), but all I knew was how happy and joyful he was, just as a dog was meant to be.

When someone gives us advice or at times words of comfort, it is not necessarily the words that matter, but the love that embraces those words. We can hear things from another that we may disagree with, but if love comes with the words, that is all that matters. It is the love then, that we feel the most. Love is the healer, the changer, and the heart opener if we are indeed ready to accept this energy. And embodying it ourselves as well as receiving it, is what will serve to create the very new world in times to come.

How can we begin to feel this new energy of the heart, and how do we let it in? Several months ago, my laptop computer decided it would not let me in. It vehemently declared I needed to change my password, but it was not password protected. And even if it was, I could not get into it to change it! Very perplexed and at that time frustrated, as I was in the midst of preparing the latest WINGS post, I called the manufacturer of my computer (I could not even get on the internet to find their number!). For what I felt was a hefty fee, I agreed to go ahead with a consultation, as I was indeed locked out with no way to get in. I will never forget the words of the technician that very easily and simply solved the problem: *"Just press enter."* It was that simple. There was no new password required, and I would not have needed to "pay" if only I had known to simply *press enter*.

My initial experience with the technician involved much detail regarding the true ownership of my computer and lots of other red tape and detailed empty calories, along with agreeing to the fee. Just like trying to clear our issues, or have a healing, or attempting to deliberately make changes within ourselves with so much work involved, arriving in the world of the heart is much more simple than that. We need just press enter with an open and willing heart. The new world is right there in front of us, but because of past conditioning, old wounds and resentments we are unwilling to let go of and leave behind, or even fears of the unknown, we make things more complicated than they need to be. If we choose, we can see what is really and truly here. And when we eventually come to see the world with clear eyes, it is truly an awesome sight to behold, let alone experience.

Near the year anniversary of my father's passing and still deeply saddened, my daughter made a comment to me. "Mom," she said. "Sollie (my youngest grandson) really has your smile now. I see it in him every time he smiles. He looks just like you." I had not noticed this before, so the next time he smiled, I gave him a good look! But what I saw was not my smile—it was my father's smile. In some ways, my grandson had begun to look exactly like my father. What grieved me the most about my father's passing, was how much I dearly missed him. He would no longer walk the earth again and I would no longer have the pleasure of his physical presence in my life. Having him with me since the day I was born, we had been close soul mates with a strong and deep heart connection, and now he was gone. There was a big hole now present that I had no idea how to fill. Suddenly all that changed. Now, when I look at my grandson, with whom I have always shared a special connection, I not only see him, but I see my father as well. He is still here, if even in a different form. And it was right in front of me all along. I had not noticed, as I was still focused on what I had lost and not on what was right here.

There is an amazing beauty that weaves itself in and out of this world, and it is here right before our eyes. After we lose so much, we then begin to see what is left, and what is left is indeed the rare and beautiful energy of the heart.

Because the new energy of the heart pushes itself out and expands after it embodies each and every one of us, we need not intentionally try and figure out what it is that we need or want to do next in our lives. Where we need to be, what we need to do, and much of everything else vital to us now, will simply *emerge* through the rubble, all on its own. Like a new and fragile flower sprouting up from a dark and barren soil, slowly and surely, our own individual *new* will reveal itself. A magical and magnificent emergence begins to occur through this new and amazing expansion, as the old world dies and the new world arrives.

If we follow the signs, and if we go to spaces that energize and excite us, and if we notice where we have "accidentally" ended up, and if we notice what is right in front of us, we will come to see that our *new* is indeed here if we only choose to see it. This *new* may only be a temporary place during the End Times, but it will always be comprised of what we need at that time and what fits us in every way. And who knows—for many of us it may be our very new heaven on earth, where we will remain for the duration of our life here on the earth.

We can ask ourselves—What makes me feel good? Where do I feel light, happy, and carefree? What energizes me, if I allow myself to go there? When do I become excited and animated? What would make me forget everything else? Where would I go, be, or do, and be willing to leave everything behind if I could? What would I do that I have never been able to do before? If I had absolutely no responsibilities, what would my life be about? If we continue to go to places and do things the way we always have, because that is what we are accustomed to by habit, we may miss something very new and different—and something that fits us much better than the old ever did.

When getting a change with my hair recently, I continued to go back to the way I had always done it. I seemed to say repeatedly to each stylist, "This is what it usually looks like. Can you make it that way?" It was only after a new stylist did something dramatically different and very drastic (absolutely *not* what I had suggested!), and after I got over the shock that it was not my norm, that I eventually came to embrace something new. And now, of course, I love it and so does everyone else.

If we are not sure what in the world now brings us joy, peace, and a sense of fulfillment (and do not choose to follow the signs), we can always pretend we are eavesdropping on a conversation nearby. Imagine one person saying to another (I will use *she* for all purposes): "Have you seen _____(your name here) lately? I haven't seen her for so long and have been wondering what she is doing now." "Oh, yes!" says the other person. "I just saw her last week and she is wildly happy doing _____(you fill in the blank, and you can get as crazy as you want!). "I would never have guessed that she would have ended up doing that and being there! I am so happy for her! It is like she is a new person with a brand new life."

Many of those who have served the planet for eons of time, have now been set free to tend to themselves and experience a life on earth that they never had an opportunity to experience before. Strange ways of retiring, removing ourselves from the old, and just sitting back and enjoying life are now at their fingertips.

As we transition through the End Times, individually and as a planet, eventually we come to find that things get much, much better. Life as we have known it leaves in slow and steady increments; we lose much, but are filled up once again with more love and heart energy than ever before. We come to know what gratitude really and truly means, and what matters most to each and every one of us—and most every time, it is the energy of the heart.

. . .

They were sitting on his porch swing. Griffin and Laura— just the two of them on a Tuesday afternoon. Griffin's boot stretched out before him, as if yearning to see something not yet in its line of vision, then pulled back home to the familiar...like a two year old not quite sure about venturing out on his own. With each push and pull of his boot, Griffin was steadily rocking them—his job for the moment, and his normal way of taking charge of their space—as always, the perfect gentleman.

"Yes, that property is still available," Laura heard his deep baritone voice speaking to the party on the other end of the phone. With a long phone cord stretching from the inside of his simple shack to their isolated place on the porch swing, Griffin could never let an opportunity for helping others slip by. The old rotary dial phone was delicately balanced on the arm of the porch swing, with a cord that reached to infinity—his comfortable version of a cell phone. He had used it forever and was not about to change now. And anyway, the idea had never occurred to him.

With his steady voice on its particular task beside Laura, and his long lean leg guiding their small ship as it rocked slowly forward, then back home, she was suddenly free to do as she pleased. As was so normal for her, she looked around at her surroundings and soaked them up. A girl raised in southern California, on golf courses, in etiquette class, and surrounded by lush and expensive homes, all she had ever dreamed about was living on a ranch in wide open spaces with nature surrounding her. Feeling the space around her, as it soaked into every fiber of her being, she felt cushioned in a world of timelessness, her cells calling out to her, "Thank you for the long, long awaited drink. We are quenched at last."

A gentle breeze was playing with the wind chimes, and their lazy clanging added to her sense of contentment. The breeze made a pathway from the wind chimes to the four small aspen trees in the front of the house, rustling their leaves as it continued on its journey. Taking up a much larger space than the house, was the red barn across the way. With weathered paint and worn wood, it stood tall and certain, not caring of its appearance, but simply knowing that it belonged there, seemingly unaware of anything but the fact that it was meant to be there and always would.

Beyond the barn was a small, elevated meadow, rising up to one of the many spectacular ridgelines of southwest Colorado. To the east spread 300 vast acres of meadow and grazing land, with two ponds and a spectacular view of the peaks beyond. The sky a brilliant blue, with the ever so familiar pillow-like clouds scattered randomly as if to the far stretches of the universe, Laura many times wondered if she was living within a postcard.

As he hung up the phone, Griffin joined her in the stillness of what had become a familiar occurrence for them—these peaceful moments together. "I'm back," he seemed to say, "ready to join you." Both of them noticed a movement at the same time, as a spider slowly and effortlessly descended from the top of the porch swing, his lifeline lowering him down with utter trust of where he was about to land. As he neared Laura's hand, he seemed to tell them, "I am on a mission, almost complete. May I join you?" With an unspoken acceptance, they watched as the spider passed through on his journey, a welcome addition to their space, a new and unquestioned presence. Turning her head toward Griffin's now present face, she suddenly became aware of how blue his eyes were, matching the blanket of sky above them, how he enjoyed the peacefulness as much as she did, and how easily and effortlessly they moved in tandem with each other.

These moments of utter contentment, of finding herself in a land so beautiful that Griffin would often call it "God's country," and of finding her soul companion, all after driving for four days with no intended destination—two miracles in one magical place, could only be the work of the divine. The California girl had come home at last.

. . .

Wishing you heaven in your heart, starlight in your soul, and miracles in your life during these miraculous times...may you enjoy your new heaven, as it is surely here.

My heart to yours,

Karen

CPSIA information can be obtained at www.ICGtesting.com
Printed in the USA
236291LV00002B/2/P